PARENT HOOD
vs
HOOD PARENT

Can a Baby Mama
Produce a Barack Obama?

B. SETFREY

Parent Hood vs Hood Parent:

Can a Baby Mama Produce a Barack Obama?

Copyright 2009 © Benn Setfrey

All rights reserved. Without limiting the rights under copyright reserved above, no part of this publication may be reproduced in any form or by any means without the prior written permission of the publisher of this book, with the exception of brief quotes used in reviews.

facebook.com/bsetfrey

myspace.com/bennsetfrey

blogtalkradio.com/bennsetfrey

twitter.com/bennsetfrey

Printed in the United States of America

SASS Publishing

Artwork and Layout by CopyWright Media Group®

Library of Congress Cataloging-in-Publication Data is available upon request.

ISBN 978-0-9742645-4-7

THE T.O.C.

I	The Intro	6
II	The Parent Crap	9
III	The KKK	15
IV	Like a Virgin	30
V	Sex Game	34
VI	Single Hood	38
VII	Exit Strategy	41
VIII	He's Really Not Feelin' You Boo	45
IX	Hood Figures	52
X	The Body Snatchers	56
XI	Baby Daddies	61
XII	Life Support	69
XIII	Hood Grandparents	75
XIV	Meet The Hood Parents	78
XV	The G Thang	89
XVI	Talkin' White	91
XVII	The Dirt	94
XVIII	99 Bottles	96
XIX	Name Change	98
XX	8 Days a Week	101
XXI	Cable Free	103
XXII	The PROjects	110
XXIII	The Rap Game	113
XXIV	Female MCs	116
XXV	Rap Dudes	119

XXVI	Naughty by Nurture	122
XXVII	The Sweetest Tattoo	125
XXVIII	Drinkin' & Druggin'	127
XXIX	Hi-Q	130
XXX	Driver's Heat	133
XXXI	Mental Wealth	138
XXXII	Shake & Break	143
XXXIII	Just For Parents	146
XXXIV	Spare the Rod	153
XXXV	Positive Reinforcement	157
XXXVI	Negative Reinforcement	159
XXXVII	P.A.R.E.N.T.	162
XXXVIII	Talk Time	174
XXXIX	Upward Bound	178
XL	Work Ethnic	181
XLI	Give Me Credit or Give Me Debt	183
XLII	Ego, Body, & Spirit	187
XLIII	Hope IS Dope	193
XLIV	And the Award Goes to …	195

DEDICATIONS

This book is dedicated to all the children who visit planet earth. You don't have to wait until you grow up to be someone great. Be great and be grateful now. Love can only live in peace. Think outside the gun.

To Damani my golden child. Your rites of passage and your brave heart will be your gateway to success. Thank you for being my SUN.

To my Mother and Father with love. Thank you for showing me the way, the truth and the light.

ACKNOWLEDGEMENTS

To Rho and Faye my left hand woman and my right hand man. I love y'all more.

To Ron and Ros Greer of Dallas, TX ~ the Protoype of Good Parents.

T. Sherie and T. Hardy ~ Thanks for being there.

My three sisters ~ Michele, Lori and Kim you are only love.

In memory of Michael Jackson. Meeting you in Vegas inspired me. Parents, always tell your children they're beautiful. It will create a postive self-image that no man or no mirror can destroy.

THE
INTRO

PARENTHOOD VS. HOOD PARENT

"Children have never been very good at listening to their elders, but they have never failed to imitate them."

~ James Baldwin

The urban expressions used in this book are for the sole purpose of reeducation. A recent study says, "*It's going down*[1] in the hood." If you truly want to educate the masses, you gotta speak their language. You won't find such words as "pedagogy" and "paradigm" up in here...up in here. Scholarly books are written for scholars.

Urban Fiction is cool, but Urban **Non**fiction is hot! You have to give the people something real they can feel every now and then. If you find slang and expletives offensive, then by all means don't listen to rap, but with all the bullshit your kids watch on TV and all the ca-Rap they listen to, like Big Mama used to say, "You gon' need some help *like-a-muhfuh*[2]."

President Obama is the Father (Figure) of our country. He wants us ~ and we need to ~ step-up our parenting game. Don't trip. If Obama said nothing then he would be turning his back on an entire community of people. I'm aware Dr. Cosby, Mr. President and I have broken the **Kolored Kode of Konduct**[3], but there is no secret place to talk to 40 million black people. Freak-Nic[4] has been cancelled. Besides, white people can see us! They know urrbody in the hood gettin' tipsy.

---

1   To party & bullshit, drink and drug, and/or spark drama
2   Bad as hell.
3   Covert bylaws that prohobit enlightenment.
4   An all black annual gathering that took place in Atlanta that was cancelled because too many black people showed up.

THE INTRO

Badass parenting separates the good parents from the hood parents. This is where kids with badass behavior come from. Children don't just look like us they act like us, too. Some parents have *dirty basers*[5] thinking. Why think like every other *ninja*[6] in the hood? There is much more to life than cash, cars, clothes, and hoes. There is a big difference between the good life and the hood life. Hood parents don't just live in the hood. Hood parents have a hood mentality and they are all around us – inside and outside of the ghetto. We can rise above hood thoughts. The intellectual and spiritual masses don't think like this.

The good news is you can change your life and the lives of your kids when you begin to change the way you think. If 66 million people can accept CHANGE and vote the only remarkable candidate into the position of Commander and Chief despite race, then hood parents can CHANGE, become inspired and mold and shape their children so that they have the confidence and courage to create and achieve greatness in their lives.

Racism may never evaporate, but the projects are vanishing with the quickness. There may be one earth, but we live in different worlds hence, the crack house and the White House.

The world is watching and waiting to see what impact the First Family will have on the urban family. The truth is, no matter what the race, if Barack Obama doesn't inspire you nothing will. Success happens. All you need is a made up mind. You gotcha mind made up?

---

5 *One who smokes crack daily but doesn't bathe daily.*

6 *Negro, Nigger, Negrito, Niggah, Insurgent, Black mattress, gym shoe*

THE PARENT CRAP

THE PARENT CRAP

Today 370,000 children will be born in America. Parenting is the most difficult job on the planet. Oddly enough there are only minimum requirements and qualifications needed to get this job. No certification or license is required, no background or security check. No neurological or psychological tests. No competency test. No education. No IQ test. No piss test. Absolutely nothing. This could be why we have parents of the corn raising children of the corn.

This is one of the drawbacks to living in a free country. You could have outstanding warrants, be on crack, and flaunt your lack of parenting skills on reality TV for the world to see, but this ain't all about Bobby and Whitney. (Although when she sang, *I Go To The Rock,* they went to the rock![7])

In this country the only things you need to become a parent are some ovulating eggs, a few drops of sperm, two (sometimes just 1) consenting adults, a Maxwell or Kem CD, your favorite drug of choice, a bottle of Patron and you're ready to hunch.

Now it's 9 months later and Cliff (pending paternity test) and Tiffany give birth to baby Cliffany. We will discuss baby names later. But now you have a ball of clay that is ready to be molded and shaped into something wonderful.

What will you create? What tools do you have to create with? How will you improve the job your parents did raising you? Will you put a man, a drug, a drink or a woman before your child? These are just a few of the questions you have to ask yourself before the lovemaking or random casual sex begins.

Although there is no legislation as to how many children one can have in the United States, in China you are allowed 1 child per family unless the first child is female or disabled. If you have more than this they fine your ass.

---

[7] *Rock as in "crack is whack" cocaine*

PARENTHOOD VS. HOOD PARENT

That's the really good thing about this country, you can have as many kids as you and or the government can afford. Parenting expertise, not so much. Today, single parent homes outnumber two parent homes. Many single parent homes got it goin' on and those families should be commended.

Far too many families, however, have been replaced with baby daddies and baby mamas, and baby mama drama. Marriage, work, and education are practically taboo. Hate and rejection have replaced love and affection. Too many fathers prefer blunts, yak, and *shones*[8] over raising their kids. It's difficult for kids to compete with crack. Crack babies are now in their 30's and have children of their own.

Today it's parenthood vs hood parent and hood parents are kickin' ass. The baby daddies are just making babies. The baby mamas are the baby makers; and the teens have been reduced to sex machines. Diaper bags are replacing book bags as we drink, smoke and cuss.

Many mothers hate the baby daddy more than they love their children. Some mothers only have children just to stay connected to the trifling father. Some moms spend more time at the *trap house*[9] than their own house. As a result, many of the children are raising themselves, not completing high school, becoming sexual active and becoming parents at a very young age. Teenage baby mamas, what could be worse? The teenage baby daddy. This is how the evolution of hood parents began and the children are the casualties of the war between them.

Teen parents and young adults are not signing up for Parenting 101 or Nurturing 102. So you have to say God bless the child and hope for the best.

---

8   *Loose females*

9   *Crack house*

Many parents say some stupid ass shit right in front of their children. Some parents can be demeaning, condescending, and mean spirited. It's bad enough to make you wanna holler and throw up both your *gats*.[10] Parents leave their children mentally, physically, and emotionally scarred, sometimes for life.

If we put all the cards on the table chances are somebody may have abused you physically, verbally, sexually, or emotionally. You're simply passing on your pain by repeating the cycle. It could be someone taught you bad parenting so you're just passing it on. Hurt ninjas ~ hurt ninjas.

Hey, people can also teach you what **not** to do. If your mother spent all her free time in jail, then you can do the opposite. "I'll give my children love and affection. I'll be there for my children." A lesson learned by turning a negative into a positive.

> *Smart people learn from their mistakes.*
> *Wise people learn from others mistakes.*
> *Ignorant people learn to repeat the same mistakes.*

You don't want to drink, smoke and curse. You don't want to get fired from your job. I know you don't want to sell dope…some dope just told you it was cool. You don't want to steal. You don't want to beat your kids. You don't want to be a hustler. You do these things because it's what you know. It's what you're used to. You pretend you're right even though you know you're wrong.

Some of you had a good life and think taking the easy trifling way out by quitting before you start is the answer. Well, it's the wrong answer.

Psychiatrists suggest that 85% of the population is dysfunctional. That figure includes parents, teachers, attorneys, psychiatrists, strippers, pimps, etc.

---

10   Guns

PARENTHOOD VS. HOOD PARENT

Only about 15% of the population is getting it right. Maybe that's why one percent of the population runs this country. The rich get richer, the poor get poorer, and lame parents get lamer. Someone please call 911.

Although you may find some of the contents of this book amusing, parenting is no joke. Some parents abuse alcohol, others smoke crack and the chances of a book making them stop is slim. But the Bible is still the best-selling book of all time. Ironically, it's also the most commonly stolen book.

Just because you don't stop one thing doesn't mean you can't start doing something positive. The projects weren't built in a day. Therefore, we need books for parents to read while they're *tweekin'*[11] and when they're sober. You have to meet parents where they're at whether that's at the after hour, the trap house or the club because it's going down.

Fathers,[12] love your shorties at least as much as you love the NBA, NFL, your butterfly doors, and *dubs*.[13] I understand your motto is Fuck Bitches, Get Money. But these do not qualify as manly deeds. I know Jesse said, "Barack is trying to tell niggahs how to behave." Unlike the Rev, instead of cutting off his nuts, I just want to say, "Thank you, President Obama for stepping up to the plate."

Parenting aint no punk. Parenting is hard work if you do it right. It's easy, if you ain't doing shit except abusing alcohol and your kids every now and then.

When you step into the wonderful world of parenting failure is not an option. It's your option if you choose to do nothing with your life, but when children become part of the equation you have

---

11 *High as Hell*
12 *Men who take care of their children*
13 *Car rims*

to step up your parenting game or your child will be lame. Your words have power ~ choose them wisely. Love can only live in peace.

THE KKK

Due to the state of the black disunion, for the first time in American history, the **Kolored Kode of Konduct** (KKK) has been unleashed. The time has come for the KKK to be shut down.

The common belief is that the powers that be make drugs and weapons available at a reasonable price in urban areas to help keep the people broke, busted and disgusted.

There's a high price to pay for affordable drugs and weapons. Despair, poverty, crime, drugs, weapons, gangs, as well as apathy plague African American communities like bootleg movies. Pimps, parents, playahs, politicians, and pastors all have to work overtime.

Recent studies show that the No Child Left Behind Act was bullshit. Act like you care about public school children then remove music, art, foreign language and monies from the school. The policy was created by the man who gave us the covert act, No Oil Left Behind.

Yes, the system was set up to hold us back, but if we're serious about keepin' it real we must admit that it's not only the government dissin' our children.

Why is it a major problem in the black community when famous, affluent black men approach a podium, step to the microphone, and stand in front of a camera and suggest to black men and women across the country that they need to step-up their parenting game?

When Bill Cosby and President Barack Obama spoke out regarding the bad ass parenting that is taking place in the black community and encouraged parents to become self-reliant and accountable, black American "leaders" ran to the KKK.

Instead of putting the spotlight on the hood parents, we got beef with the Prez and Cosby for going against the KKK. Only in the black community can you be criticized for Enlightenment. *Ninjas por favor[14]*.

Check out the Kolored Kode of Konduct in black & white:

Article I

Persons of African descent are prohibited from discussing the problems in the black community publicly or in "mixed company" unless they are blaming "the Man" or a non-black person for the problems the black community faces.

Article II

If anyone of non-African decent, white folk specifically, speaks ill of the black community publicly or in earshot they must heretofore be immediately labeled a racist. It doesn't matter if the accusations are true or false. In case of emergency or when in doubt pull the Race Card.

Article III

If a person of African decent from the hood speaks publicly about the issues in the black community to a crowd that is less than 101% African American and blames the black community for their own problems, even if true, he or she shall immediately be labeled a "sellout." If said person uses standard English he shall also be accused of "ackin' white" and "talkin' white."

Article IV

If an affluent, educated African American who doesn't have street credibility publicly speaks ill about the black community, even if

---

14   *Niggahs please*

true, he or she shall henceforth be labeled "sellout," "removed," "elitist," "not-in-touch," or a "bustah!"

Article V

If an African American who is 50% black speaks publicly to a diverse audience and encourages parents to become self-reliant and accountable, his remarks shall be deemed condescending and his nuts shall be cut off post haste by a man of the cloth. Rev. Jackson has the right of first refusal.

Article VI

Whenever a hate crime is committed that involves a white person and a black person or whenever police brutality allegedly takes place, you must immediately run to the "black phone" and call Reverend Al Sharpton. Unless there's traffic, he should be there before you hang up with his hair fried, dyed and laid to the side.

Dial 1(800) MANE-MAN

Article VII

All persons of African descent who choose to publicly denounce the use of the word "nigger" may do so and may still continue to use derivatives of the word "nigger" i.e.:

> Negro (Negro, please),
> Nicca (That's my nicca!),
> Niggaz (Deez niggaz crazy) or
> Niggah (I'm through with that niggah)

However, they must solemnly swear to only use these words in the company of black friends and black family members. White people shall continue to use "Nigger" covertly in the privacy of their own homes even if they have street credibility. This includes Paul Wall, Bubba Sparxxx, and Marshall Mathers aka Eminem.

Article VIII

If you are African American and happened to pastor a predominantly black church, praise God. You shall have dominion to pimp your parishioners. Aman! They shall purchase you mansions, Maybachs, Bentleys, furs and jewels all in God's name. In exchange, the pastor must guarantee salvation and a free eulogy to the members of the flock.

> ***Disclaimer***: *Faithful tithe payers only. Must be saved and speak in tongues.*
> *Hotta-ham-anda-balowny-and-cheeseha!*

Article IX

Whenever any African American who has celebrity, whether he be athlete, singer, pastor, etc., commits murder, rape, larceny or any of the 7 deadly sins, you must stand behind him until Jesus comes. This is a black thing no one else shall understand.

Article X

No educated black person shall ever speak to any reporters on camera as eyewitnesses. You shall be ignorant. You must be wearing a *wifebeater*[15], hair must be braided, a mess or covered with your favorite rag and you must preferably have missing, brown or gold teeth.

Article XI

Whenever a heinous crime is committed and the media does not announce or print the race of the alleged perpetrator(s) you must immediately join hands with nearby African Americans and pray the suspect(s) is not black. If there are no other African Americans in your vicinity, then you must discreetly pray silently.

---

15   *White tank top dudes happen to be wearing when caught on tape beating their wives on the TV show "Cops"*

THE KKK

If you're an atheist or agnostic and choose not to pray, you shall clap your hands and sing the Negro spiritual below as a reminder.

Hell is a hot place ain't no water there
I said Hell is a hot place ain't no water there.
No water where? No water there
No water where? No water there
I said Hell is a hot place ain't no-no-no-no-no
Ain't no-ain't no-ain't no-
Ain't no water there!

The KKK is pretty cut and dry and rarely ever violated due to fear of *"blacklash*[16]*"* Many black people and black leaders in general don't like it when black people discuss the problems of the black community in "mixed company," when we're blaming ourselves for the problems at hand. If we are blaming white folks then it's cool.

The question is where should this covert conversation with over 40 million African Americans take place? Wednesday night Bible study? The Circle City Classics? The Tom Joyner cruise? There's no way to get that many black people on a ship again without chains or an open bar. The last time that many of us boarded a ship we went through the door of no return.

I gotta secret KKK members - **White people can see us**.

We're not invisible! They know we like to party like a rock star while in poverty. It kisses away the pain. They know the roof is on fire and we don't need any water because we're going to let it burn. They sing it, too, while dancing off beat. "Burn motherfucker, burn."

Yezzir! I'm blowin' the whistle and ringin' the alarm. And-What?

---

16   *When ninjas attack*

PARENTHOOD VS. HOOD PARENT

When white people fuck up all hell breaks loose. We let 'em have it publicly i.e. Don Imus. We checked the shit out of Imus. It was all over the airwaves. Everybody and anybody with a drop of black blood shut him down. "That white racist mutherfucka needs to be fired and have his nuts cut off." And that was the black clergy. Imus will never talk about another nappy headed ho again and if he sees Superhead coming he's gon' run the other way.

The KKK generally takes the hands off approach. We have a way of whuppin yo ass like Rodney King without touching you.

Now when WE mess up publicly …. Anybody else hear crickets?

When the Rev. Jackson called the future president a niggah it was a hot topic for about all of five minutes. Jackson even broke his black "CAIN'T SAY NIGGAH NO MO" vow. These were two good reasons to rip Jesse a new one, four if you include fathering a child outside your marriage and not avidly supporting Barack. But we swept it right under the rug. (KKK Article IX)

If the Rev. Jimmy Swaggart had called President Obama a nigger, ninja please! Swaggart would have been beat down and fucked up.

We can get away with murder. But not stealing our stolen shit back. Ask O. J. Karma is a bitch!

Now I'm not saying he did it, because I can't, he's black and I'm black and this would be a violation. (See KKK Article IX)

Besides he was found not guilty, which doesn't mean innocent by the way. But come on people; we've talked about this in the privacy of our homes and friends' homes for years now.

Chris Darden, the black prosecuting attorney cried us a river, but y'all didn't give a damn. He was black too. But he wasn't "celebrity black." We loovvveeee celebrity black.

We'll come together and rally around R. Kelly when he allegedly bumps, grinds, and pisses on a teenaged girl even if it's caught on tape. It's the "Who you gon' believe me or your lying eyes" defense.

We're sympathetic for the teenage girl, but we don't know her like that and she's not celebrity black so we have to defer to KKK Article IX and support the black celeb. To the teenaged victim, holla back lil mama when you get a record deal.

What can Brown do for you? Ask Rhianna, she even supported Chris "the black celeb" for allegedly whuppin her ass for poppin' off at the mouth. You know the KKK is powerful when you forget you're the damn victim.

We police the white folks when they screw up, but nobody is policing us, but the police. Where the hell is the village?!

The lack of parenting that's going on today, seriously, WTF. Who is policing that?

Too many kids and adults are turning into unfit parents and they need to be checked. Yet, black folks trip when Mr. Coz and Mr. Prez attempted to educate and enlighten them.

Our people need super father figures to uplift us. It seems like some people get in the way just to shake shit up because it's not them leading the way. Fall back and stop hatred. Many are called, but few are chosen.

So we have to keep it real. The KKK is killing us. Those of us who still work or live in the hood know there is some shady shit going on in our community and we look the other way. Bootleg cable is one thing, but beating down a human being in the street because they're homeless don't make no damn sense.

PARENTHOOD VS. HOOD PARENT

It's time out for crossing our fingers, praying and hoping the perpetrator on the news is not black. (See KKK Article XI)

We need some preventive medicine. An idle mind is the devil's workshop…Is anybody still teaching this?!

We are committing stupid ass crimes because we got too much free time on our hands. You can remember to bring a gun to school, but you can't remember to bring a damn pencil?!

The bad news is we have run out of excuses not to make it in this country. The scale is not balanced, but you can't keep a good man down or back.

The good news is that even though racism is alive and well, the cream rises to the top. Confidence, conviction, and charisma go a long way. We now know there is nothing a black man cannot achieve in this country despite white skin privilege and white supremacy.

There are no more reasons not to make it in America in the midst of all the racism and prejudices that still permeate our society. Even if the system, the public school system specifically, is set up to hold us back, WE have to be hyper-vigilant with raising our kids. "Party like a rock star" is not the Jewish community's anthem or secret to success. Don't forget they had a holocaust too.

This may mean we can't drink and drug everyday and that we have to actively raise our children. Read a parenting book or two. Routinely visit our children at school so we won't have to visit them in jail. Get educated. Get a job and keep the job. Stuff like that.

If we could get parents to support their children like we supported Barack, O.J. and R Kelly we would be Jewish. We would have future physicians, attorneys, and presidential candidates in the making. We would be running things. The word on the street is the original Jews were Black. But before you say, "Mazeltov my niggah!" we have some work to do.

The mere fact that Mr. President, a black man, can obtain the popular vote in the United States of America has to be a wake up call for every ethnic persuasion on the planet. He received the Democratic presidential nomination. The only thing bigger than this is Serena's hump. This is black history, American history and a spiritual victory. I smell a national holiday coming.

The only thing that sets the Prez apart from many other black men in the hood is good parenting. His mother and grandparents were self-reliant and accountable and so is he. This is what his Father's Day speech in 2008 was all about.

He said, "Too many fathers are MIA, AWOL abandoning their responsibilities and they're acting like boys instead of men…more than half of all black children live in single parent households. Children who grow up without fathers are:

- 5 times more likely to live in poverty and commit crimes.
- 9 times more likely to dropout of school and
- 20 times more likely to end up in prison, have behavior problems and become teen parents."

The question is…was he lying?

He wants parents to assume the position and become responsible and reliable parents. This ain't offensive. He's just keeping it real, but you can't keep it real and piss off the KKK simultaneously.

Values can be positive or negative. Too many (not all) people in the black community have negative values, clinging to crime, cruelty and badass parenting.

PARENTHOOD VS. HOOD PARENT

The values that should be fostered are love, compassion and wisdom. Slavery has ended. Now what's up? Do you wanna raise a Toby or a Kunta Kente?

Black people need what's called determination to succeed. When an overweight black woman from the south can rise and become America's Queen of Talk and the highest paid woman in television, and when a black man from Anywhere, USA can rise and become the Leader of the free world, times have changed ladies and gentleman.

We have overcome!

The United States of America has elected an African American man as Commander and Chief. This is bigger then Aretha's bra drawer.

We have overcome!

We say we believe in God, but we act like the devil. If you don't enjoy life then do the same thing you do when you're spending hours in front of the TV ~ Change the channel.

You're the dealer. You're in the driver's seat. You're walkin' it out in $200 sneakers. If you're broke, busted and disgusted that's your fault.

We have overcome!

Dr. King predicted it. What he didn't predict is that his kids would be suing the shit out of each other. But I digress. Black people now have crazy opportunity. If you don't believe me ask Flava Flav. If he can make it and make a comeback!!!…well you know the rest.

Someone has to be brave enough to say publicly, "Step-up yo parenting game." Cosby and President Obama may be removed but I'm not.

Benn Setfrey? I hear you singing Rapper Dolla's joint *Who-the-Fuck-is-That?*

I'm from the hood. I worked for Chicago Public Schools in the hood. Milwaukee Public Schools in the hood, and Miami-Dade Public Schools in the hood. During my tenure, I've worked with children from K through 12. I've worked with pregnant teens and teen parents. If my finger ain't on the pulse, then it ain't no pulse and there ain't no hood.

Who else besides a black man, black woman or Jesus of Nazareth could give constructive criticism to black parents for being apathetic and triflin'? No other ethnic group would be allowed to do it without being labeled a racist. (KKK Article II.)

What's race got to do, got to do with it?

Many of us find being hood fab more important than being intelligent. Our heritage is important to a large extent, but our level of spiritual awareness and common sense is even more important. Your spirit is color free. It's time to transcend race and communicate on a spiritual level. Our spirit is above and apart from this material world.

The truth has no race, creed, or color. Therefore, if John McCain told black, brown, yellow, red and white women alike that tattoos on the neck are not a good look that's the truth. It doesn't matter what color the messenger is when it comes to the truth. What's more important is their intention.

The Reverend Jackson accusing Mr. President of talking down to black people is ludicrous. What about the Black people that routinely talk down to their children? Who's going to defend these children?

PARENTHOOD VS. HOOD PARENT

Super Crackman, Ms. Crackman and Baby Crackman ain't offending nobody?! They need someone to show them the way, the truth and the light.

We gotta save the children so education will be valued as much as snitches get stitches.

It's bananas when you really think about it. We are so divided and separated by race, religion, and politics that we can't even focus on the reality at hand. Gas is higher than Bobby Brown and too many people are becoming parents who act like good parenting is taboo. Perhaps, the baby is not the one the doctor should be slapping at childbirth.

A good child may be hard to find because good parenting is even harder to find. There are no bad kids. There are children with bad behavior because of badass parenting going on in communities of every race, creed, and color.

Often times behaviors, good and bad, are learned directly from the parent(s). The nut doesn't fall too far from the nuthouse.

Since some parents, not you of course, are unconsciously spoon-feeding your child dysfunction everyday you should consider indoctrinating your child with the right stuff, baby.

Newborn babies need new and improved parents. Ignorance and stupidity are not legitimate defenses for producing crack babies. Most ignorant parents, unfortunately, won't admit they're ignorant. Some don't know they're ignorant, which means *they know not that they know not*. Therefore, Ignorance is Bliss, blind, deaf and dumb, too.

Well-mannered and respectful children are not born they are created. This book deals with the norms, not the exception. We all know some children are good babies, infants, toddlers, adolescents and decent human beings in general. But they are not typically the norm. It's time to develop our parenting skills on the front end. Then there is less jail time on the back end.

Perhaps you made several bad choices prior to becoming a parent. Maybe you were drunk and/or high and said to yourself, "I wanna go half on a baby." Then the next thing you know you're pregnant. Then you smoked cigarettes, mary jane or crack while pregnant and around your children, abused alcohol, did meth, X, used obscene language toward and around your kids, and remained unemployable.

Brittney and Anna Nicole have already proven that sex, drugs and procreation don't mix. Why reinvent the crack pipe?

Many people think they are having a baby, but you're having a human being who will one day become an adult. You don't want this adult to become an incompetent member of society and a piss poor parent. Do you?

So your little ball of clay should not be treated like a little ball of $hit. Clay is moldable, shapeable, and ready to be nurtured as soon as it comes out the womb / Shit stank. So the question is what type of parenting skills do you have in your arsenal?

In the '60s we watched Leave it to Beaver. In the '70s we tuned into The Brady Bunch and The Jeffersons. In the '80s the world watched The Cosby Show.

Martin and the Simpsons replaced the Cleavers and the Bradys. Though the Huxtables showed the world that upper class families of color existed, people chose to emulate Martin, believing the Huxtables were make-believe.

The series 24 cast a black man as leader of the free world several years ago and the series Commander and Chief placed a white woman in the oval office. People said it would never happen in a million years and look it took less than a half billion seconds.

PARENTHOOD VS. HOOD PARENT

President Obama and Hillary Clinton made history in 2008, turning fiction into fact and changed the face of what the President of the United States looks like. By doing this they have given a new generation of children and adults inspiration. Miracles will never cease and if Dr. Cosby and Mr. President can't break the Kolored Kode of Konduct, I will.

LIKE A VIRGIN

PARENTHOOD VS. HOOD PARENT

Congratulations you're a virgin! Millions didn't make it, but I'm glad you did. It's a good thing you've taken time to read this book before you embark on parenthood or stumble across a life threatening STD. There's a lot you need to know about sex before you jump on or let some dude jump in.

One out of five teens are confusing love with sex by age 14 and 1/3 of American girls become sex machines and are pregnant by age 20. The most important thing you need to know is everybody might hate Chris, but everybody loves virgins from high school seniors to high school dropouts, from pedophiles to Planned Parenthood.

VIRGINS BEWARE & BE AWARE! You're America's sweetheart and America's Most Wanted. So you have to be extra careful because a lot of ninjas are going to be in your ear and trying to hit your sweet spot. You have to be very careful lil' mama because the dude you let deflower you might also defame you. There's a lot you need to know about sex before you spread your legs or let some ninja hit it from the back. The main thing you need to know is teens make better virgins than parents.

People will pay to be entertained sexually and there is a billion dollar pornography industry to prove it. Rapist don't rape for sex, but for power over their victims. Pedophiles are in it for the seduction. Statistics show that the people having the least sex are married couples. Well they may be having sex, but just not with each other.

The professionals or the people in the business of selling sex will tell you it's really not sex their customers are paying for. I've spoken to a Geisha - a woman trained as a professional companion for men - or two and they will tell you that their highest paying customers aren't really paying for sex, they're interested in having attractive companionship with good conversation without commitment. Yezzir! People will pay good money for you to go away. Ask Paul McCartney or MaDonna.

Be careful my dear sweet virgins, some dudes will tell you they want to be in a relationship just to get to your hot spot and by the time you slide your thong back over your possy, he's black history. Don't fall for the *okedoke*[17] or lame *game*[18]. Sex might get him, but sex won't keep him. If it's marriage you want then you must fish in the right pond. One good sign is meeting a man who has parents that are married or were married at length. If he has parents that value marriage, then there's a good chance he may also.

Remember many men and women don't know what marriage is. All they know is that most of the time it eventually ends in divorce. Chances are you may not know a lot about marriage either so how do you learn? You learn by reading about what makes relationships work and what doesn't. Meeting someone you can develop a spiritual partnership with should be your goal. Then you will have someone you can grow and develop with spiritually. Peace and harmony will then be your focus inside the relationship, not power and control.

When women relax and show no interest in commitment, men commit. But when women pull the marriage card, men freeze, choke and head for the door or to the next female's door. Attempting to make someone your possession is the last thing you want to do. Establish a friendship and they'll keep coming back for more.

You need a humble, considerate and spiritual man, and of course, you need to possess the characteristics that you are looking for in a mate. "Crazy" trying to meet "Sane" will not be a match made in heaven. So before you start hunchin' try crunchin' on what's on the next page.

---

17   *Lies dudes tell to get the buttocks*
18   *Lies dudes tell to get a piece of your cherry pie*

PARENTHOOD VS. HOOD PARENT

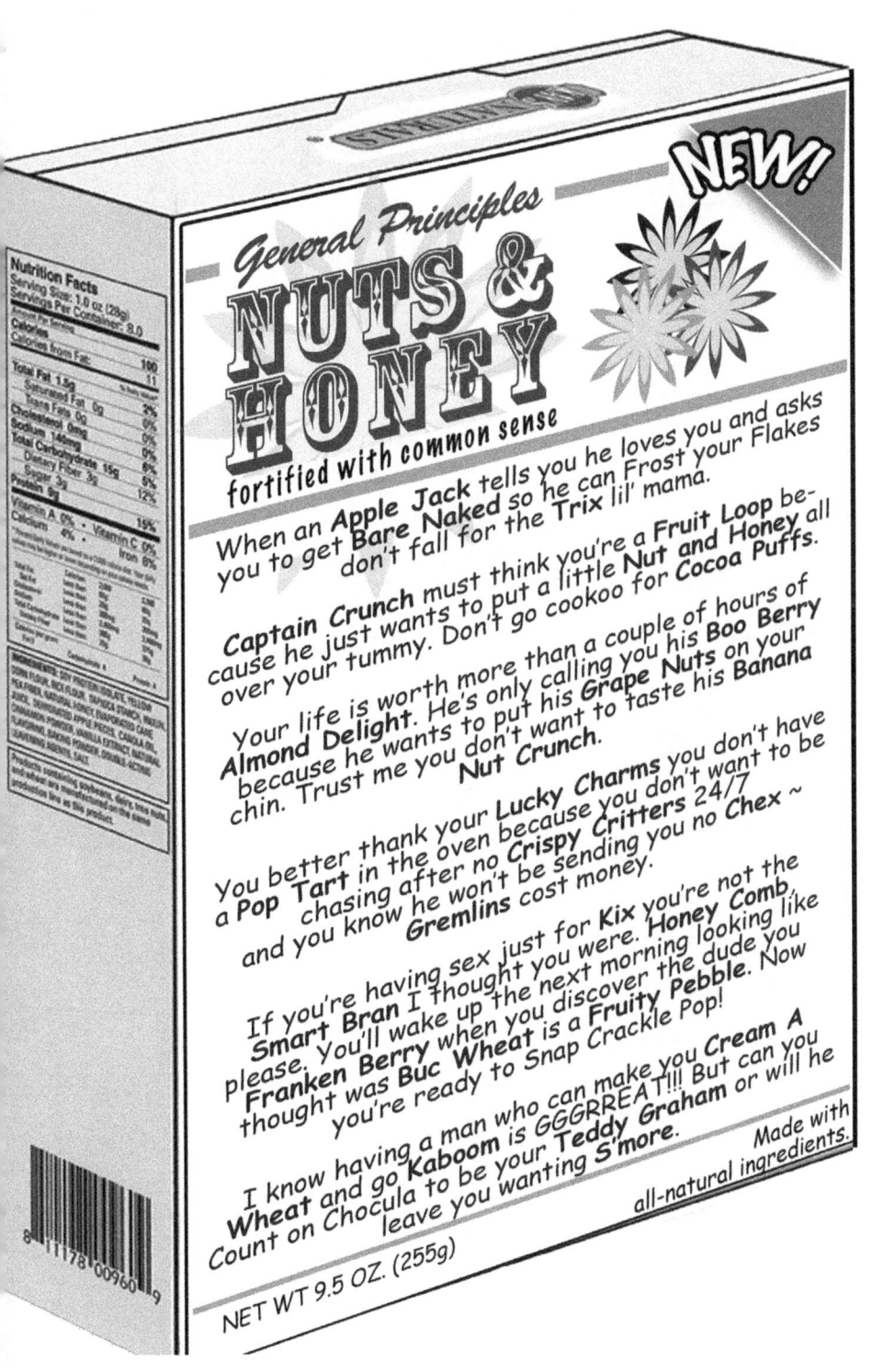

SEX GAME

OK so your sex game is tight. And-what? Are you making love or taking love?

It's hard to believe that we live in an era when something that's so good to you can actually kill you. Yezzir! HFCS, not High Fructose Corn Syrup, Hot Freaky Casual Sex. This is the only thing sweeter and deadlier than High Fructose Corn Syrup.

Sometimes I wonder if the people who are just out there having random sex have ever made love inside or outside the bedroom. The people who are addicted to sex are never addicted to making love they're addicted to taking love. That's why they feel empty when they're not sexing someone up or stroking them down so they continuously go out and search for their next victim. You can't form an addiction from making love because making love is natural and has nothing to do with intercourse and more to do with *outercourse*[19] and unconditional love.

Whether you're making love or taking love, babies can be a byproduct. So, like Salt-N-Peppa, let's talk about sex baby.

What is it about you that makes sex so enjoyable, so addictive and causes you to become so insatiable? Is it the body contact? The orgasm? The comfort of a man or woman? A man's or woman's touch? The way he or she makes you feel? The freak in you? The lack of self-love? Loneliness? Co-dependency? The man's worth? The woman's worth? What???

---

19   *Sex without penetration. The opposite of intercourse.*

SEX GAME

Now if you don't have a high *libido*[20] this may not apply to you. But many people will kill and do die for sex. Making it clap ain't so sexy once you get the *clap*[21]. There are new and convenient ways to find sexual partners and love that never existed before. You don't have to get dressed or put on makeup or weaves anymore. Thanks to the Internet you can meet people in cyberspace and have *NSA*[22] intercourse as much as you want. It sounds official, but it's artificial.

But is sex enough? Would you rather make love? It took me months to figure out what the acronyms on the Internet dating sights stood for: ISO (in search of), NSA (no strings attached.) The list is endless.

> *His sex may be good,*
> *and your body is bad*
> *You're not ready to be a mother*
> *and he doesn't want to be a dad*
> *Girls today go from learning*
> *ABCs and 123s*
> *To having STDs*
> *and multiple baby daddies*

Young adults, older adults and children are advertising on the 'net, too. Many of the women are looking for love and many of the men are looking for NSA sex. Ladies, I have a secret, if men, like dogs, could perform fellatio on themselves the marriage rate would be even lower. So we need you more than you know.

One in 4 teens have an STD. This includes thugs. I know *shawty*[23] want a thug, but Herpes, HPV and HIV, Chlamydia, and Gonorrhea

---

20 Sex drive
21 An STD.
22 No Strings Attached.
23 *A sexy young lady; Tenderoni. A bad, bad bi-otch*

likes thugs and thugettes, too. There are so many bugs lurking under foreskin, in pubic hairs and in the vaginal and anal walls just waiting for you to slide in so they can attack your genitalia. So if you prefer unsafe sex, ladies and gentlemen, you're risking your life. Dum da-dum dum dum!

Now let's say you are dumb enough to take the risk, which usually means drugs and alcohol are parts of the equation. Inhibitions get very low when you are under the influence. This simply means when you get drunk off your favorite poison you don't give a damn what happens in the bedroom, closet, basement, attic, couch, chair, floor, table, counter top, desk, park, bathroom, airplane, train, car or bus. Instead of thinking I haven't tried it there yet, think I'm going to protect myself and not make a stupid ass decision I must live with for the rest of my life.

SINGLE HOOD

PARENTHOOD VS. HOOD PARENT

When is the last time you have been truly single? No Booty calls. No friends with benefits. No, "I gotta do this so he'll pay my cell phone bill." No Nothing.

You don't want to spend the rest of your life with you but you think somebody else does? Wrong? I know what it's like to wake up in the morning and there's no one there snoring next to you. Your man left you. So what! It is what it is, accept it. Ain't your mother every told you, "You can't keep no man that don't want to be kept." Hello?!

Say it out loud ladies and gents. HE IS NOT MY POSSESSION. I DON'T OWN HER. SHE IS NOT DEAD. I DON'T OWN HIM. I FORGIVE HIM, I FORGIVE HER AND *"I FORGIVE ME."* (One of my favorite poems by Rhonda Swan.)

Most men and women are looking for possessions, not spiritual partners. When the sex gets old, then what? When the toe starts to jam, then what? You need somebody you can grow and develop with on a spiritual level. You want peace, but you start shit. It's time you realize drama doesn't find you. Fill in the blank. You find _____. You know the word because you're used to it.

People who are at peace don't have drama in their lives. This is life. You're not playing cards. When somebody asks you who's your baby daddy and you got one and two possibles…this aint spades lil' mama. Play the cards you're dealt or reshuffle and deal yourself a new hand.

Your child ain't but two years old and you have had three live-in boyfriends, none of whom is the baby daddy? You can't have random men around your children. Some people who you might trust with your no good judgment could possibly be untrustworthy and sexually molesting your child and you won't even know it until it's too late.

This is another benefit to singlehood. You help keep your children out of harm's way. Trust no man and not all women with your children to a large extent. Shy away from sleepovers unless you're present. This is not an attempt to make you nervous or paranoid, but you need to be conscious and aware at all times. There's nothing wrong with erring on the side of caution. Remember family members are suspect, too.

Having a partner is not a badge of honor. Being single is not a death sentence. The truth is that the same people who are not happily single will not be happily married.

EXIT STRATEGY

EXIT STRATEGY

Rule number #1: Children First. If a man is whuppin up on your ass or verbally abusing you or your children it's time you put your kids first. Get O-U-T. Men only do what they believe they can get away with.

Have you noticed only punks hit and abuse women? Let a man step into the picture and they're ready to talk. What did Kanye say? "The only thing I wish is a niggah would."

One ass whuppin is one too many unless you provoked it. Listen, that means you don't get your ass up in no man's face talkin' shit, putting your hands in his face, cursing him out and by all means don't hit him first. Legally he can defend himself. Yeah a man may say, "If you try to leave me I'll kill you." Hello! He's killing you softly anyway, Ma. If you don't have a father, father figure, step-father, uncles, brothers and cousins to protect you, as the saying goes, "In God We Trust." Fear no evil. Never sacrifice your dignity for the sake of a man.

You shouldn't be in a relationship where your significant other is always poppin' off at the mouth. You're a parent first. Kids don't need to see or hear this shit. What I'm saying is don't enter into verbally and/or physically abusive relationships. If you discover after the fact that you are in hell's kitchen that means you didn't do your damn homework before you got pregnant.

Some young women get pregnant by dudes they have known less than a month. This is some dumb shit, and I say this with love. You don't get pregnant by a dude and you don't even know his government name. This would make you a fool.

A lot of men will pay for sex. On a good day dinner and a movie, too. A lot of women will pay for love. Don't get me wrong it's OK to cater to your man. Beyonce said it. She didn't say financially support your man. "You need your car note paid? Ok boo. You

PARENTHOOD VS. HOOD PARENT

want an iPhone? I gotchu boo." Then you find yourself boohooing when he's gone.

Don't cry over lame dudes when they decide to leave even if they did father your child. Peter, Paul and Mary would consider this a blessing. Now, if a good man and provider leaves you for another woman or man; cry me a river. I understand, Mami. But there comes a time when you gotta dry your eyes with your child support check.

Exhibit A: *Kim Porter, Puffy's baby mama. Ching, Ching gettin' paid over here.*

But Pooky from down the street, who ain't got a pot to piss in or a window to throw it out of? If you shed a tear it's a crying shame. Keep it pushin' lil mama and count your blessings.

Ladies, men may cum and they may go so invest your money on your children making sure they have the things they need. No, not the new Jordans. For instance, a magnet, choice or private school.

EXIT STRATEGY

When a man leaves you, forget slashing tires, hate mails, posttraumatic stress texts and stalking. In case your mother or father never told you the pursuit of happiness, excellence and success is the best revenge you can ever have. Some people expect you to fall, fail, and freak out when they leave you. I say fool their ass. You cain't keep no ninja that don't wont to be kept. We all know if you were making six or seven figures the dude would be right there waiting for you to flush so that he can wipe.

The last thing you need to hear is any Jennifer singing "And I'm telling YOU!..." So turn off the radio that's full of sad ass songs. Turn on your gospel music, read your daily affirmations, talk to God and visit friends and family, focus on your children and remember nothing helps you get over the last one like the next one. In a word, REBOUND! And by all means workout! Get your body tight.

If I called the people I'm seriously involved with (in my head) every time I thought about them a judge would restrain me for life. You don't hear me. The time has come for you to break-up, breakdown and breakthrough.

HE'S REALLY NOT FEELIN' YOU BOO

HE'S REALLY NOT FEELING YOU BOO

"I don't wont nobody but you."
"I love you like Soul Food ma."
"Ay bay bay, I wanna marry you."

Relationship experts would call this bullshit. Yeah, he's got a hot ring tone, but where's the ring ma? You have to be able to identify a bogus negrito before you see him cumin'. Stop playin' the nut role.

> *"I wont you to have my baby."*
> Translation: "I don't like using rubbers."
>
> A dude will tell you anything he thinks you want to hear in order to hump on your *camel toe*.[24]
>
> *"I love you and your stretch marks girl."*
>
> Don't fall for the lame ass game lil' mama. The first thing in the morning dude might say, "You fine as hell." Come on now - you gotta mirror. Although you may be beautiful on the inside, the first thing in morning … you look like a man.

Single ladies, What's cracka-lackin'? MEN are smarter than Women?! I didn't get the memo. I thought women claimed to be smarter than men on anything to do with sex, love, relationships and spending money that ain't theirs. Wrong!

Not in the bedroom. Ladies you're *slippin*.[25] I don't know who told this lie. You can't blame this one on Bush. It's one thing to be slow, but when you're "George Bush" slow, ladies you have real serious problems.

---

24   *An imprint that is formed when women wear tight pants that resembles a camel's toe.*

25   *Not focused. Losing ground.*

PARENTHOOD VS. HOOD PARENT

I heard pimpin' ain't easy and that it's hard out here for a pimp; but if there were no hoes there could be no pimps. Pimps would be forced to: sell their own ass for cash; use their lips to earn *chips*[26] and keep their pipe hard - to pay that Master Card. Seriously ma, *WTF*[27]?

How can so many of you fall for the okedoke over and over and over again. These lines are all getting old and lame and, if you're falling for it, so are you. You ain't even climaxing over and over and over again.

Game is supposed to recognize game. Ain't it?

Women are smart, but dudes are slick and greasy.

I hate to use the word "all". But deep down *all* men think *all* women want to be married. And not just married, but married to them!

Now ladies you know this is not always the case, but some of you act so damn desperate what is a man left to believe.

Stalking is not sexy and desperation is not a good look. Ya *feel me*[28]? So desperate some of you are willing to be with a man at whatever cost. For instance, your man is making babies outside the relationship and bringing STDs inside the relationship, and you accept it.

Never compromise your dignity for the sake of a man. Leave the insurgent where he stands. Look lil ma, single ladies and baby mamas…if you play by these new rules you'll never be hurt again by a man who loves you or who doesn't love you.

---

26 *Money.*
27 *What the Fuck.*
28 *Understand*

IN GENERAL THE AVERAGE MAN LOVES:

Some dudes also like to spend time with family and friends and have a little random sex on the side.

Fuckin' is in the fabric and in the fiber of a man.

Women need to see a visual aid to understand why the man of your dreams may really be the ninja of your nightmares.

Some men are addicted to sex and you might as well face it *PYT*[29]- you're addicted to love.

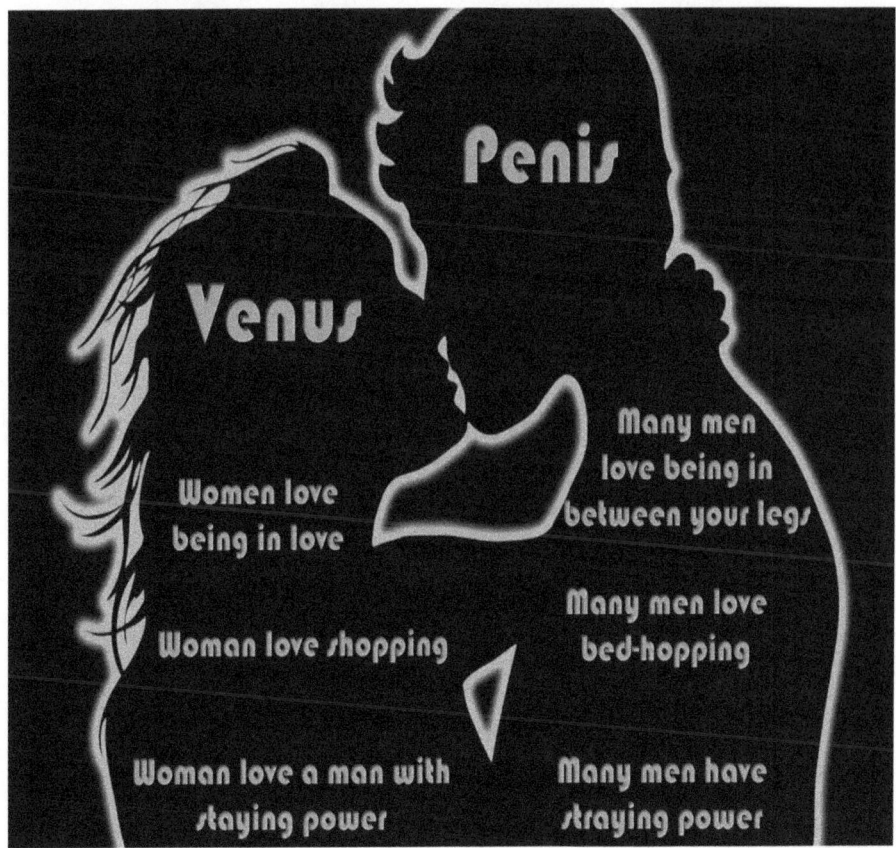

These rules apply to all tax brackets; ask Halle Berry. In Halle's defense, not that she needs one, but she tried every shade of Negrito from damn near white to telephone-black. There ain't no seven figure African American albinos running around Hollywood; so she had to cross over. Interracial dating beats interracial hating any day of the week.

Some men do have staying power. They go to work everyday and come home every night. They're faithful, spiritual and wise. But these men are not looking for a baby mama and her drama. These

---

29   *Pretty Young Thang*

men are looking for a sophisticated lady with class, not a hood rat with a big a$$. They want a sanctified lady. Hallelujyer.

In general, men think you want to get married. And in general you do. This is merely classic conditioning. Sleeping Beauty, Cinderella, and Princess Jasmine are partly at fault.

You grew up watching the Disney Channel and I Love New York. Put them together and you have the ~~not so~~ Wonderful World of the Ghetto ~~Fabulous~~.

Due to the lethal combination of the Ghetto & the Fabulous, ladies shouldn't be pissed when your beautiful, black or brown, professional brothers turn to Snow White or one of the 7 dwarfs for comfort. No man in his right mind is bringing lil' fabulous home to meet big mama.

Ladies, you also have to be sure to look at the object of your affection with your spiritual eye not your black eye (~~Rhianna~~). Is the shining armor that your knight is wearing a pistol? If so, the next armor he might be sportin' may be handcuffs. Clank -Clank.

What your soul really yearns for is someone to help you grow and develop spiritually. And you do this by gaining peace and understanding before you enter in a relationship. Don't begin looking for all of your mate's faults and none of your own.

You believe your guy is bipolar because he acts bipolar. I got a secret lil' ma…you have the same behavior. You have issues too, boo. But because your eyes are wide shut you can't see yourself. You see only what your body's eyes show you.

After you unplug from the matrix you will awaken and be able to stop judging others because you will be too busy spiritually perfecting the gorgeous lady in the mirror and loving your Self.

PARENTHOOD VS. HOOD PARENT

It takes a certain level of wisdom to get to this place, but once you do, it will change the way you respond to your date, mate, your children and your Self. You will begin to think wisely before you speak. Then and only then will you notice people are now responding to you on another level because what you see is a reflection of your Self - good or bad. Dream Girls.

HOOD FIGURES

PARENTHOOD VS. HOOD PARENT

Yeah lil' mama, a little swagger and street cred may be wassup, but they don't go a long way. If having a soldier boy is at the top of your "To Screw List" then I hope you wrote your list in pencil.

Your sweet prince of the ghetto needs to understand the definition of true and real before he claims to be a trill niggah. Trill niggahs don't lie, cheat or steal. Trill niggahs do trill things.

Ladies if you want to keep it **trill** you have to start now.

You have pipe dreams of marrying a doctor and you haven't taken your GED test yet. It's not going to happen lil' mama. Your mind is playing tricks on you.

Baby mamas and hood mothers-to-be; you now have no excuse. You've been put on notice. You now know that there is a good chance your baby daddy or future baby daddy may not know a damn thing about fatherhood.

Yes, he's hood fab but I know there comes a time in every woman's life when you stand in the mirror, after your high comes down, and you say to yourself, "Damn! I need Lipo."

Then you say, "Damn, I chose this lame a$$ muhf#@ka to be my baby daddy? WTF was I thinking?"

The reality is you picked the *fuck niggah*[30].

If you have already spawned with a hood figure, then it may already be too late hood mama. Don't waste your time being miserable and living in regret thinking you would have been better off if you had dropped, gave him *50*[31] and swallowed instead – uh…yeah?! But you can't cry over spilt *leche*.[32]

---

30   *A triflin' womanizer who lives off you.*
31   *Head*
32   *Spanish word meaning milk. Also Spanish slang for semen.*

HOOD FIGURES

Is your dream for your unborn son to be a baller, a shot-caller, or a playah? I know you want him to be hard that's why you punch your toddler in the chest and slap him in the face and say, "Stop actin like a punk, bitch!" All that is ~~not~~ fine and ~~not~~ good. All the time and energy you spend making him hard; you could spend time to make him hardworking, too. A strong work ethic goes a long way.

Use caution when you choose a baby daddy. "He phyne" is no longer good enough. If your *shorty's*[33] papa is a rolling stone your child is going to want to imitate what he sees. Especially when hood parents make drinkin' and druggin' look so damn good. To put it mildly - TV, music, movies, and video games are fuckin' little boys and girls up in the head.

Frederick Douglass would be pissed. And if Harriet Tubman had a drop of blood left in her body it would be boiling.

The only thing you try to read shouldn't be somebody else's mind. Some people think if God wanted them to read, He'd send them a text.

Why read? I could think of about 60 million reasons. That's about the number of African people who were annihilated during the middle passage and human purchasing (slavery).

If that's not enough, I've got 400 hundred more reasons. This would be the number of years black people were not allowed to read, and were tortured, beaten and killed if they were caught trying.

So if you can go day in and day out without picking up a book, then *do you* and watch bullshit reality shows day in and day out. Who am I to judge?

---

33   *Typically refers to a male or female child*

PARENTHOOD VS. HOOD PARENT

But if you begin to feel too like *ish*[34] it would be a great idea to read to your children and or have them read to you.

Whatever you do most you will be best at. If you play with your Wii all damn day, then you will be the best in the hood. If you devote time to raising children the right way, then you will create brilliant children.

Hood mamas, you can't be shocked if little Ray-Ray, who raised himself for the majority of his life, grows up to become nothing. The concrete raised him. The same streets that might have raised you and your hood figure.

---

[34] Shit

THE
BODY
SNATCHERS

PARENTHOOD VS. HOOD PARENT

I've worked with teen parents and pregnant teens and it's unanimous. When a boy, guy, dude, gentleman, thug, young man or old ass man tells you they want to make a baby with you and they love you, what they really mean is they enjoy raw sex. They don't like the way condoms feel and they could give a damn about you or the child they may be creating or the STD they may be bringing or receiving.

Wake up girls, ladies, shawtys, older women, buss downs[35], runners, and shones. Men show love to get sex and many of you are giving sex to get love! It don't work that way, ma. You can't make a man love you because you got good sex, good head and a bad body. If you offer a man sex (pleasure) and expect love (joy) you're bananas (touched).

Some teens and grown ass women tell themselves, "I'll get pregnant on purpose that way he'll always be a part of my life." WRONG! While you are busy getting pregnant on purpose he has moved on to the next female.

Have you checked the number of single parent homes? Men are not looking for kids to raise (including their own). They're looking for pleasure when they get hard and you must be ISO pain.

Now if being a sex machine is what you're signing up for then ~~not~~ cool. You're about as bright as a blackout and I say this with love.

Just think about it. You wash your hands before you eat and after you use the restroom. You shower before work and/or bed. You squat to piss when using a public restroom and you avoid touching the door handle on the way out. All of this makes sense. But then you go out and lick foreign penises like they're la la la lollipops. Baby, I'm scared of you.

Dix love two things:
1. *bang bang bang*
2. *skeet skeet skeet.*

---

35   *One who gives free fellatio and enjoys it.*

THE BODY SNATCHERS

Many men want to do the right thing but the dix are runnin' things. Dix can't be trusted to only cum home to you. That's why we call them dix. They're dumb, like to cum and usually attached to a bum. You didn't get the text?

If the man loved you and himself he would become...

I – N – D – E – P – E – N – D – E – N – T

Do you know what that means?

PARENTHOOD VS. HOOD PARENT

Aint no *cribbin'*[36] at yo mama's house jumpin' off. I can't understand sex first then ask questions later. Ask questions first:

If he says, "I'm in between jobs" that's one good reason right there why he should NOT be in between your legs.

You have to ask the right questions:

> *Do you have any children?*
> *Have you been tested? HIV tested? Drug tested? IQ tested and other STD you can think of.*

Be specific. Don't worry about ruining a mood. Your mood might be ruined for the rest of your life if you go sit down in the restroom and your vagina falls in the toilet. STDs ain't playing with yo ass, penis, mouth or vaginal area. Touch yo neighbor and say, "I don't know where your ding-a-ling has been."

There are some people intentionally going around spreading diseases because they are mad at the world. The world ain't done nothing to you. You didn't screw the world, although you may have tried.

---

36   Living.

No one but yourself affects you. You need to wake up and realize you're creating this life. Hood-rats are not born they are created just like top models.

This is where the rubber meets the road. If you don't have any idea how much it costs to raise a child from 0 to 18 there's a pretty good chance that you should not be hunchin' without a rubber. If you want to know how much it costs to raise a child, visit:

www.babycenter.com/cost-of-raising-child-calculator

Remember thugs have STDs, too, even the fine ones. They're getting mo' ass then a lil' bit. If you are dumb enough to let a dude run up in you without a rubber then I'm gon' tell you like Usher, Let it Burn.

One out of five people who have HIV don't know it because they have never been tested. It's ok to love hunchin' but if you are doing it with every Tom, Dick or Harpo, it's important to remind you that's nasty and dangerous.

So having unsafe sex is really like putting a bullet in a revolver, spinning it, aiming it at your private parts and pulling the trigger. If dix were good and wholesome we wouldn't call them dix. Dix can't be trusted they have a head and a mind of their own - that's why they're always looking for *brains*[37]. Kind of like the Scarecrow in *The Wizard of Oz*.

Your man loves you. His dick loves to fuck. So don't be a dick. If the man behind the dick is good and wholesome, put him in a box and sell him on Ebay to the highest bidder or marry him your damn self. If you really like partying like a rock star and fuckin' like a porn star it's important to remember you can't screw when you're dead.

---

37   *Slang for fellatio.*

BABY DADDIES

BABY DADDIES

People are still trying to figure out what came first the fried chicken or the fried egg. The real question is what came first badass kids or badass parenting?

No child is actually "bad." Though he or she might have bad behavior, those behaviors are learned. Habits are developed. And sense ain't common. So before you sip on your Syzrup, and before you pick up your first or next blunt or maybe even a crack pipe, meth or X, you should consider abstaining from sex, particularly unsafe sex because when the smokes clears you may spawn children that you and/or the world does not want.

Badass parenting produces badass kids. It's like a crapshoot, you never know what you're going to produce; a President of the USA or the pimp off MLK. Genetics play a big part.

Pedigree is more important when it comes to making puppies than making babies or so it seems. What kind of stock are you from? If we authenticate animals' pedigree, we should check out the future baby daddy's or baby mama's pedigree before the hunchin' begins. It's not a good idea to hunch with people with bad genes. The rubber he might wear might break.

If you have bad genes consider adopting a pet. If you find yourself cursing your dog or cat the fuck out, pass on the kids and thank me later.

Your future spouse or baby daddy needs to be *vetted*.[38] Shopping for good pedigree simply means check the family out for any history of mental illness, multiple incarcerations, obesity, lack of education, and any severe allergic reactions to full time employment. Shit like that.

You should also do some fact finding to determine if there's any history of gold teeth, or lack of teeth. It's important to do a

---

38   Checked out

PARENTHOOD VS. HOOD PARENT

background check before you begin hunchin'. Sex is one thing, producing children who may be predestined to go to prison is another.

Lets take a look at biological fathers (also known as baby daddies, sperm donors, and triflin') who choose not to parent their children.

Baby daddies are the primary reason we don't have more little Michele and Barack Obamas running around. If being absent or getting missing is the only thing you can do well as a parent, then your children may be better off. After all, no influence is better than bad ass influence.

There ought to come a time in every man's life when you say, "Dayum!" and just start kickin your own ass. Delusions of making it rain[39] in the club with your one-dollar bills. Dollar bills that really ain't even yours because you ain't paid child support since Jesus was a baby, Burger King was a prince, and the Pope was in preschool. If Rick James, God rest his soul, was here he'd tell you, "Pay yo bills bitch." Your shorties gotta eat, too.

Let it be said to the baby daddies that are doing it right, Don't go around bragging by saying stuff like "I take care of my muhfuckin kids and I buy them shit." This makes you sound crazy as hell and you may not be. Leave room for doubt.

You're doing what you're supposed to. "I take care of my kids." Who's supposed to take care of them, me? The government? Brangelina? You know they love random kids.

Only baby daddies and baby mamas want to be rewarded for caring for their children. I don't get it.

---

39 *When wanna be ballers throw dead presidents in the air at nightclubs.*

Don't get me wrong. It's a good thing you do care for your children because we know many don't. However, there are parents who go the extra mile. They go above and beyond the call of duty. Soccer moms, music lessons, karate practice, annual vacations, super sweet six-teens, *quinceaneras*,[40] quality time, acting classes, tennis lessons, they read books together, yes books. The good parent list is endless.

All that said, a woman can't be mother and father. A man cannot teach a girl how to be a woman or a lady. A woman can't teach a boy how to be a man. She can be the best damn mother possible, but it takes a man to step up to the plate and father his son.

A woman can teach her son how to survive the encounter with the police. "DON'T GIVE THEM ANY REASON TO SHOOT YO ASS." It's "Yessuh, Mr. Ocifah." They have a license to kill.

But men teach Manly deeds. It's difficult for fatherless boys to perceive and embrace fatherhood. Why? They've never experienced it and rarely see it!

Fathers have the responsibility and obligation to take their sons through a rite of passage once they reach adolescence. No, not the typical night of blunts, beer and big booty bitches at his superdupa sweet sixteen.

The problem is since you're ghost your son is forced to substitute his rites of passage with gang initiation, affiliation and gang related activities. They teach him that the test of a man is measured by having the ability to shoot somebody and feel no remorse.

The real test of a man is having the ability to remain humble when you're up against the wall. Honor, respect, character and dignity go a long way. Once you ruin your name and credit what are you

---

40   *The Latin version of super sweet 16 that happens at sweet 15*

really left with? Criminal minded, gun charges, probation, and felonies are not wassup.

You never know what a man is made of until he faces adversity or life's challenges. Do you give up, give in or keep it pushin'?

You can be a self-made man and still earn an honest living. Ask college dropout Bill Gates or single-parent home-dwelling Barack Obama. Judge Mathis is a former high school dropout and gang member who did jail time as a juvi.

Your dream of being the next Godfather or Fred Lucas is no different from Mike Tyson dreaming of hosting the next Miss America Pageant. It's wrong on so many different levels.

You're living in fairytale-land trying to get out of project-land and before you know it you end up in court-land and wakeup in prison-land. The next thing you know, you're a *buss down* and dudes are paying yo' prison pimp cigarettes to hunch on your booty. *Saggin'*[41] is now something you no longer want to do.

Check it out playah, shortcuts don't last long. I know quick cash is your answer and I would agree with you if more black dudes were in college than in jail.

Since that's not the case, I gotta put my money on my man Malcolm X:

"Education is our passport to the future."

School is your enemy because you didn't do shit when you were there. You ain't stupid, academically you just don't know nothin'. So you use double and triple negatives like I just did and break verbs without even knowing it.

---

41   *Pants that hang below the buttocks to tease gay dudes.*

Yeah you're nickel slick, penny wise and street smart and I know this is helpful behind bars, but what about when you get out? Free your mind before you're locked down and locked up.

The old *heads*,[42] *OG's*[43] in lock up and yo grandma nanna want you to know when or if you go to jail the first time it's supposed to be a wake up call. If you don't wake up it could be because you wake up high everyday so listen to whatever guidance your gifted relatives and friends give you.

Pretend you're hearing this for the first time:
- Go back to school.
- Stay in school until you graduate.
- Finish what you start.
- Stop quitting and quit stopping.

The old heads have been getting their hustle on longer than you. You're listening to these young kats with billion dollar dreams and federal nightmares. You better wake up. The world is in you. You're not in the world. Your thug life and spiritual life are clashing. Change what you do and you can change what you see around you.

Man-Up Brothers, Bruthas, and Hermanos. We have a job to do that no one else can do but us. Many women don't want to be the head of the household. They become head of household by default or by yofault. Ladies would love to have a man who is responsible enough to step up to the plate. A woman would love to have a man who goes to work everyday and comes home every night. Even the *ABW*,[44] they still want a partner to share their lives with. Believe it or not they depend on you to bring out the peace within. They sometimes forget to turn to God, so allow God to work through you.

---

42   Elders

43   Original gangsters

44   Angry Black Woman

PARENTHOOD VS. HOOD PARENT

The only thing worse than a young ass trifling man is an old ass trifling man. Going pro and a rap career is cool if it happens. But nobody is going to discover you on the neighborhood playground hoopin' it up. Most talent scouts are scouting at high schools, colleges, and universities. If you dropout, your hoop dreams are now a nightmare.

If rapping is what you do then you need to find a record label and become an intern. Keep writing. Keep rhyming and stay true to the game. Make it your hustle. Make hits.

Jill Scott said she got a part-time job painting the lobby at Jazzy Jeff's studio. She would just be humming her ass off while she primed and "polyurethaned." She hummed the tune *Is It The Way You Love Me* very loudly everyday until she got an invite by a producer into the booth to sing. That's hustle.

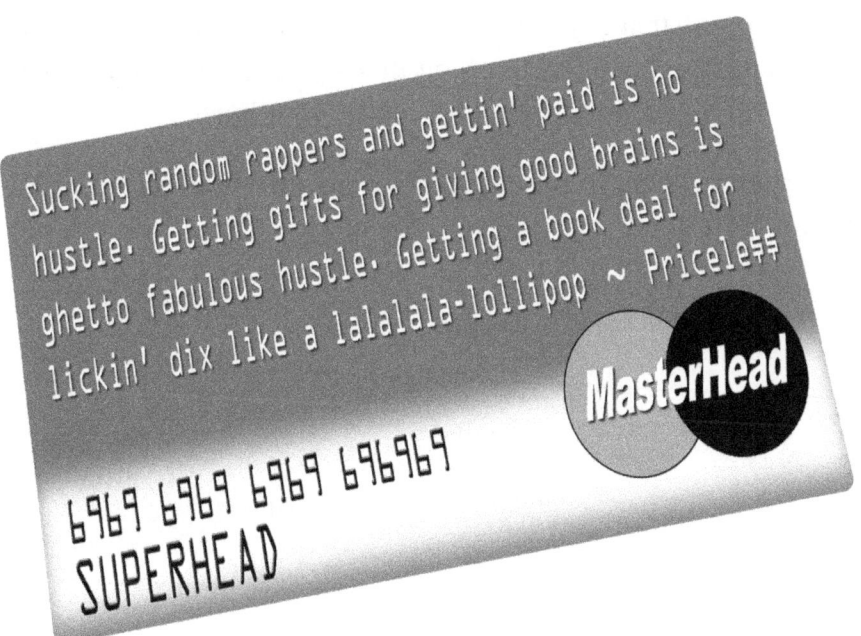

When you sell dope, that's not hustle. That's called helping to kill off the people in your community.

If you're not part of the solution, you're part of the problem.

So you need to get your head right, this is what hustlin' is all about. Not this short-lived shit going on in your ~~not so~~ friendly neighborhood. You still have to work. You still have to maintain. You won't find out what hustlin' is really like until you do time at an *HBCU*.[45] If you make it there you can make it anywhere.

So it's cool to have a Plan A: rapper, producer, pro ball player. You also need a Plan B, attorney, teacher, pilot, physician, mechanic, electrician, waiter, etc. Unless you're willing to make your Plan A your hustle. There's always work at the post office. It's good to remember you won't be discovered sitting on your mother's couch playing PS2.

Whatever you do most you'll be best at. So if you play your Wii day and night that's your hustle. If you spend several hours a day on FaceBook or Twitter, then that's your hustle. If you get a scholarship to play ball, then that can be your hustle.

The secret is when you're workin' on yo' shit it doesn't feel like work. It feels good.

---

45   *Historically Black College or University*

LIFE
SUPPORT

LIFE SUPPORT

So you discovered you're in love with *Becky*[46] all by the tender age of 16. Women are bitches, girls are hoes and (biological) kids mean as about as much to you as chocolate on a toilet seat.

You hate your own sperm donor for not being there for you so you go out and create fatherless children of your own. Do you see the cycle repeating itself or is it just me and the rest of the world?

Children cannot effectively raise themselves. So if you are going out dropping your seeds and leaving your children for the streets to raise, then in your own words, "that's some bullshit" and pretty fucked up. Raise your own shorties.

Asshole muthafuckas and stank-ass bitches are not born, they are created. This is the house that crack built and/or the lack of good parental role models.

If you think it's cool to sock your 4-year-old in the chest because he's playing on the floor and say, "Get yo punk ass up off the floor!" then you don't have what it takes to raise kids. It may be better if you don't fuck up the next generation, too. Because verbal abuse, getting children high, physical abuse and neglect is not wassup. And it ain't funny even if you don't ask me.

Some would consider you dumb as hell to turn your kids on to drugs and alcohol and they ain't even out of elementary school yet.

Now some of the dangers you face with having sex in the raw besides giving and receiving STDs is the possibility of having an unwanted pregnancy. Which means two words – child support.

---

46   *Really good fellatio*

PARENTHOOD VS. HOOD PARENT

**Seriously, who should pay for
YOUR CHILDREN to EAT?**

Trust and believe that it will be just a matter of time before the department of revenue's office catches up with you and when they do, if you are the non-custodial parent (NCP), you've got more than hell to pay.

Check out the poster on the next page.

THIS LIST SHOULD BE POSTED ON YOUR SON'S BEDROOM DOOR next to his Scarface poster:

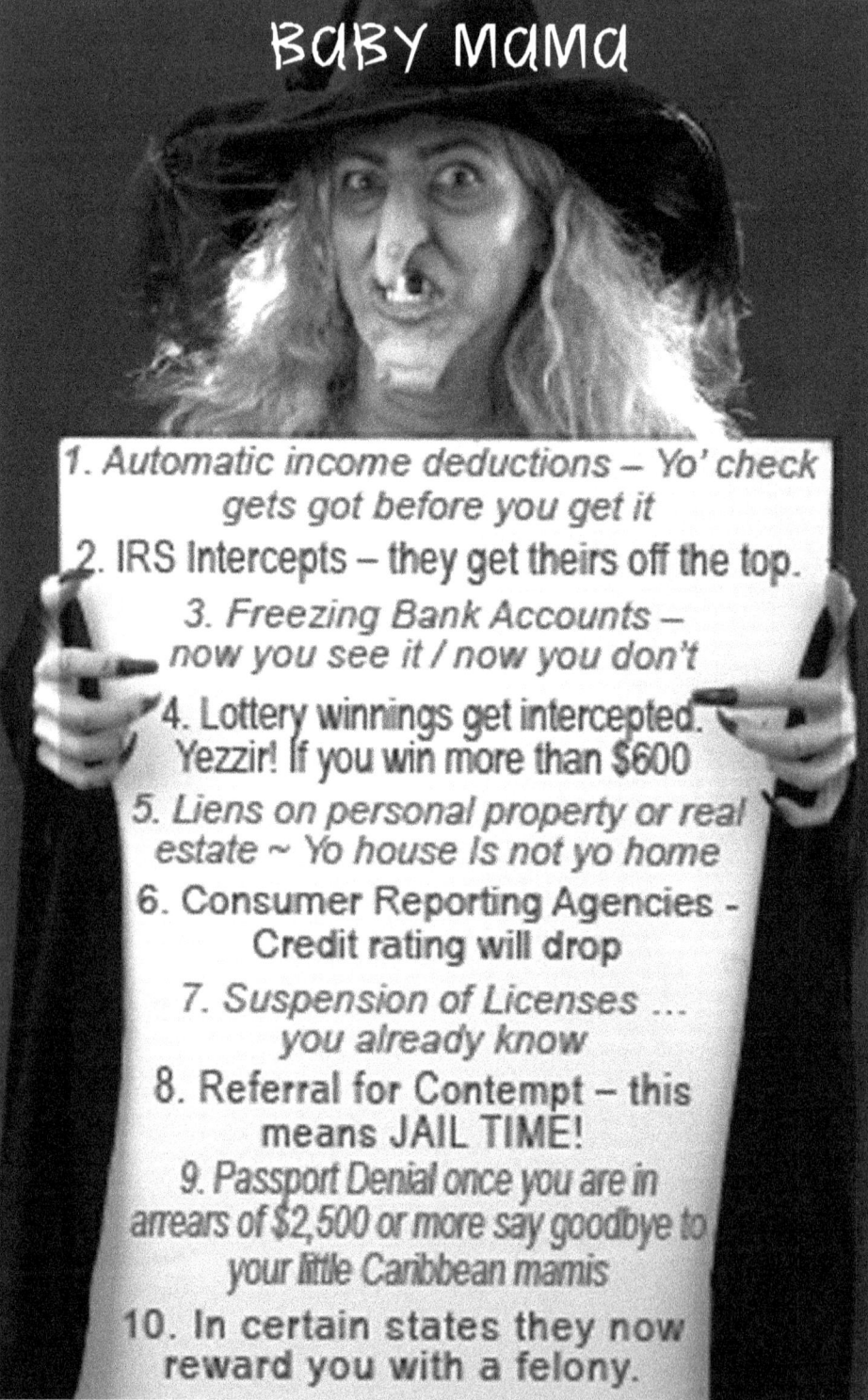

PARENTHOOD VS. HOOD PARENT

Rappers should start rapping about this in between rapping about fuckin' bitches and getting money.

The hidden message here is wearing a little bit of latex can keep you out of a whole lot of financial trouble. It has also been reported that condoms are not stopping you from feeling anything during sex. You might have just got caught with the short end of the *magic stick*.[47]

The other message is, as my big mama used to say, "If you don't want to pay chile support stop fuckin without a rubber. These chirren didn't ask to be here. You'll wish you had used a rubber when you go to sit down to use the toilet and yo dang-a-lang fall off and is floatin in the toilet next to yo bowel movement. These STDs is serrus as cancer honey. God help you witcho dumb ass."

Believe it or not, most men don't like paying child support because they believe their baby mama is going to get her hair and nails done with the money. This is a weak ass defense for not taking care of your shorties and not paying child support. My answer is put a damn rubber on if you don't trust yo' potential baby mama with money.

Calling your baby mama anything but her government name is bogus. You *boostin.*'[48] Fighting and cursing in front of your shorties is a punk move. Never slander any woman and especially the woman who gave birth to your spawn. To use your words, "You on some dumb shit." If you want to create the next Barack Obama, Hillary, or Michelle Obama you have to start early. If somebody called your mama a stupid ass bitch you would be pissed.

---

47   Dick

48   *Trippin' or buggin'*

This may be difficult to comprehend, but baby mamas are mothers, too. They have feelings, too. No matter how ignorant they appear. Even if they say some shit that appears to be dumb as hell like "you cant see yo baby if you don't pay me child support." Some women don't know they should contact the state and not hold the child hostage.

> *"Mothers you have to love your child more than you hate the father. Your child or children deserve the love of both parents and all grandparents."*
>
> *~ Judge Judy*

HOOD GRANDPARENTS

HOOD GRANDPARENTS

Hood parents it's not all your fault. Those sexy, little 30 something year old hood grandparents are also partly to blame. They invented *ghetto fabulous*[49] and personified it.

In most cases, you're a victim turned perpetrator. Unfortunately, once you reach the age of majority (18 and up) no one sees you as the victim any longer. You're the perpetrator unless you break the cycle, bicycle, tricycle any cycle you can find, break that *mug*.[50]

If you're not sure whether or not you're a hood grandparent, it's factored by your age upon delivery of your grandchild. If you became a grandparent before your 50th birthday you're circumspect. Say ho!

If you became a grandparent before your 45th birthday you're lookin' pretty hoodish. Say ho, ho!

If you became a grandparent before your 40th birthday you're no doubt a hood grandparent. Say ho, ho, ho!

If you became a grandparent before your 30th birthday you're a hood ass grandparent. Say skank ho…Somebody scream!

The only really sad part here is as a hood grandparent:

1. You're proud of it, and

2. You expect compliments because you look so young to be a hood ass grandparent.

Hello, you don't look young; you are young and some would say dumb, too. At 34 you're still calling random numbers in your man's phone to see who Tamichael is. Doing drive-bys to see where your man is, and allowing dudes to call you bitch and ho. You're not

---

49 *Beauty that vanishes once you step a foot outside the hood.*
50 *Motherfucker*

fully cooked yet. You're still evolving, while fighting females for fucking your rooty poot, punk ass man.

Hood grandparents the only way you can begin to break this cycle is once you have become a hood grandparent you stop having babies yo' damn self. If you allow your teen child to have a baby while living in your house understand that you now have enough children under your roof.

Fact: When teens become baby mamas and baby daddies the baby is at a greater risk of growing up to become nothing. They ain't got no damn parenting skills. You can't put people in command who don't know what the hell they're doing. Bush spent eight years proving this.

MEET THE HOOD PARENTS

PARENTHOOD VS. HOOD PARENT

Let's keep it trill hood parents. Many of y'all don't even like kids. You like them when they're at school. I mean you love them because they look like you and can pass you your cigarettes or a beer. But after that it's a wrap.

It's important to remember ignorant parents can produce more ignorant kids. So it's more important that you and other hood mamas don't welcome your children to the hood life. Therefore, it's necessary to develop some parenting skills that will have your child shoot for the moon instead of just shooting for the hell of it. Ya feel me?

Think about it, your behavior was learned. You might have been born in the hood, but you were not born hood. That tattoo above your ass ain't yo birthmark. There was no stripper pole in your crib. Yo mama didn't name you bitch.

I know it's just something you and your girlfriends call each other, but your children are listening lil mama. They think bitch is your government name.

Remember just because you're **from** the hood you don't have to be **of** the hood. When you became pregnant with your baby did you say to yourself I want my daughter to be a pretty ass ho, bad bad bitch, or a sexy muthafucka?

Then why would you make these comments about yourself in front of your child? "Sshhit, umma bad bad bitch." You ain't Trina, Lil' Kim or Foxy Brown. Stop dropping it like it's Not and pussy poppin' on a *handstand*[51] in front of your children. You're doing it so I have to say it.

It probably wasn't your parent's wish for you so why would you want it to become your daughter's wish for herself. Kids need

---

51 *A stripper dance move whereby you flip upside and make your possy clap.*

to dream bigger than this and dreams begin early in life. Infants dream of crawling, walking, talking and being nurtured.

Big Mama always said, "It's one thing to be a fool, but you don't have to be a gotdamn fool." Then she would slap the shit outta you. But some of my own relatives, former students and their parents never got this memo.

I never got the memo that said your newborn baby needs a pair of Jordans. He can't even crawl. He can't walk. He can't hoop, jump or dunk. You buy the Js and a Sean John outfit and you cross your legs and light your blunt like your job is done or as Bush would say, "Mission Accomplished," after six weeks of being in Iraq.

Now don't get it twisted baby mamas and baby daddies come in a variety of races and ethnicities, white, black and everything in between. But if you never had the pleasure of meeting one face to face, well, to put it mildly, you've been blessed. However, I will paint a portrait of a baby mama for you in case *Octomom*[52] ain't enough.

Case Study:

> *This baby mama kicks tail*
> *This baby mama been to jail*
> *This baby mama got beef*
> *This baby mama got grief*
> *This baby mama got drama*

This is a story about Nina, the epitome of a baby mama.

Nina is the mother of three, raising two, who works at a local flea market on 79th Street in Miami, FL.

---

52   *A chick who had six kids she couldn't afford then had a liter of eight that she couldn't board.*

PARENTHOOD VS. HOOD PARENT

I had a bad feeling about Nina, not because she worked at a flea market; not because she was sporting a nightcap on her head cocked to the right; not because she was sipping on a rum and coke she purchased from the ice cream truck man in the parking lot and not because she looked like Harriet Tubman about the feet. The Underground Railroad pedicure is not a good look.

She had a very hoodish look. She looked kind of like an unattractive Celie from the Color Purple. But since I don't judge others by their physical appearance I sat down in her chair and she *hooked me up*.[53]

About a month later when the time came for me to get my hair done again I discovered she was fired from the shop and banned from the flea market for boxing at work.

I couldn't start all over again trying to find someone who could hook me up just because lil' mama got a temper so I followed her to the next spot; another flea market.

Baby Mamas are typically ABW so this wasn't new to me. The fact that she was in her second trimester and still fighting was somewhat new. Nina actually had four physical altercations that I know of. One during each trimester and one shortly after giving birth.

After she told me about the third trimester fight I had to say something. My conscious was getting to me. It couldn't just be all about my hair, but you have to be careful how you introduce a subject because baby mamas are extremely defensive.

I was also getting tired of bouncing from one flea market to the next, each time some new drama jumped off and I was concerned for her unborn child, too, so I simply told her, "I read somewhere

---

53   *A good deal*

that fighting in your 1st, 2nd or 3rd trimester may harm your unborn child." This opened the door for her to tell me about the drama:

"These females be tryin' me. I went to McDonalds and my son had an accident on 'hiself' and this female who work at McDonald's was going around telling people my son was a *flea market baby*[54]. So I couldn't get at her on her job so as luck would have it I ran into her at Shoe Time (~~2 steps below Payless~~) as she was coming down the aisle. I said, hey sweetie. She tried to get around me but I didn't move so she bumped me and that's when I grabbed her and slammed her on the floor and started hitting her in the head with a shoe from the rack. My baby daddy pulled me off her before the police came. Hey, charge it to the game." (First trimester).

Now in her defense she didn't get banned from the second flea market, her son did. Jay-Jay was banned from her place of employment due to hyperactivity and piss poor parenting. He was about three at the time. Prior to the flea market filing a restraining order on her little shorty, I remember an incident with her son when things did get a little out of control.

Jay-Jay wouldn't stay seated and he eventually started a fight with another shorty he knew. I think it was his mom's play sister's son. She had tried a variety of intervention strategies at different intervals to get him to stay seated before and after the fight.

Strategy 1	She backhanded him in the mouth several times after he began to cry from being grabbed, yanked, snatched and shook. *(Before the fight)*
Strategy 2	She tried ignoring him. *(Before the fight)*

---

54 *An unkempt/untrained child, born out of wedlock, who lives, eats and sleeps at the flea market while the baby mama works kinda hard for her money.*

Strategy 3	She slammed him in the chair a few times *(Before the fight)*
Strategy 4	She pinched the shit out of him repeatedly. *(After the fight)*
Strategy 5	She beat him across his body with a heavy wooden brush. *(After the fight)*

Surprisingly, none of these strategies worked.

Her girlfriend, who was the mother of the boy Nina's son had been fighting with, had a similar discipline style. But she handled things much quicker and a little different after the fight broke out. She simply slapped the shit out of Jamarcus in and about the face and head several times hard as hell and then balled up her fist and said to him "Sit yo muthaf*#kin a$$ down and shut yo b!tch a$$ up."

Where the hell is Child Protective Service when you need them? Jamarcus had a lot of aggression after the vicious attack by his mother, but you couldn't see it on his face because his hands covered his face for about 10 minutes after the assault. He was approximately six years old.

I was happy as hell when Nina's baby daddy finally showed up. Getting your hair twisted doesn't normally raise your blood pressure, but mine was raised and boiling. I needed to exhale, but I exhaled too damn soon.

When Jay-Jay sees his dad he jumps up out of the chair to give him a big hug and baby daddy says, "Go sit yo lil' muthaf#@kin a$$ down boy and throws him in the chair. I thought to myself, "Damn, can a toddler get a damn break and some love." This boy has taken more blows in one day than Clinton did during his entire 8-year term.

Lil' dude would've been safer hanging out with a Catholic priest. So shorty gets up again after remaining seated for about two to three seconds and runs between his dad's legs for comfort and nurturing. Instead baby daddy knocks him in the head and chest and slams him in the chair again.

This cycle continues about 15 minutes. He continued to push the boy away from him until he realized the boy was not going to move. The boy was starving for love, affection, a bath, a haircut and dinner.

Baby daddy was there to get the key to the room they were renting. They were moving before they got evicted from the tenement because she had a fight with this girl out front the previous night (Second trimester).

When the "rent man" came to the flea market to find out what happen she simply told him her truth.

> *"Well, I'ma tell you da truth.*[55] What had happened was this female was all in my baby daddy face talkin' shit and he don't fight females so I walked up and axed her what the problem was then after that she got slick out the mouth and she had a bottle in her hand and she looked like she wanted to hit me with it so I grabbed her and slammed her on the ground.
>
> Then after that, I grabbed her wrist and banged it against the curb - see I got cut right here (pointing to her wrist). Then after that we tussled for a minute. When she got up she ran to her trunk and grabbed a tire iron and hit me across my back. Then after that, my baby daddy got it out her hand.

---

55   *A bold face lie always follows this statement.*

PARENTHOOD VS. HOOD PARENT

I know I'm gon' have to move so my baby daddy is cleaning out the place now. I don't really like everybody in my business, but umma go ahead and tell you. I'm pregnant and I can't be dealing with these little girls."

The "Rent Man" showed no emotion. He said he wouldn't tell the police or the girl where she worked, but she should be careful. He then asked what happened to the girl's car windows.

She said, "Oh, um I'm gon' tell you the truth.* I aint got no reason to lie. What had happened was I broke out her car windows 'cause she like to get slick out the mouth and hit people with weapons. She wanna threaten somebody so hey, she got what she deserved."

In Nina's poetic words, Hey, charge it to the game.

Nina would also be considered a *ride or die bitch*.[56] She loved her hood figure. The same hood figure who jumped her during her last trimester when she suggested he get up off the couch and get a job. He was arrested for assault.

I told my girl Nina I wasn't looking forward to her taking maternity leave, but I understood. She said, "I'm not taking no time off. As soon as the navel thing fall off I'll be back at work." I said, not "cool."

The last time I was at the flea market the po-pos raided the booths that sell bootleg designer clothes and all the bootleggers had to flea. I think that's how the "flea" market got its name. I thought they were shooting a movie. If you haven't been to a Miami flea market, add it to your bucket list.

The following scene is NOT fiction. It is being retold for enlightenment only.

---

56   *A bitch that will kill or die for her ninja.*

KUNG-FU FIGHTING

CHARACTERS: Nina, Jacky (Asian store owner), Jay Jay, and Ninjas (Nina's co-workers)

INTRO: Nina's son Jay Jay is accused of petty theft at the flea market. He allegedly stole a ball from the dollar store inside the flea market. Jay Jay spends about 7 hours a day at the shop unsupervised (opportunity) so it could get boring day in and day out without anything constructive to do (Motive).

Jay Jay is now 4 years old and unkidnappable, but this is no reason to unleash your child on unsuspecting ninjas at the flea market. (I don't believe any child is bad, but lil dude would've been safe at the Neverland Ranch). When Jacky approaches Nina at her booth to tell her Jay Jay stole a ball from his store this is what pops off next.

NARRATOR: Jacky enters the shop booth. Hip Hop music blasting. (T.I. Whatever You Like. Ninjas bouncing)

JACKY (to Jay Jay) Where yo modder?

Jay Jay (pointing at his mom and looking guilty): Right dere.

JACKY (with Chineses accent and attitude taps Nina on the shoulder): Yo-son stole my brall from store

NINA (startled and high): What?! What the fuck you talkin' bout? Man, my son ain't stole shit.

JACKY (pointing at Jay Jay as he bounces the alleged stolen ball): Yo-son stole my brall. You need pay me 1 dollah!

NARRATOR: Nina gets out of her chair and stands in front of Asian

KUNG-FU FIGHTING
(cont.)

NINA (walking up on Jacky and lying):
I ain't payin you shit. He got that ball from my girl. She said she bought it fo him.

JACKY (pissed and irate): You punk bitch I want my money!

NARRATOR: Nina backs up a couple feet and hacks and spits on the Asian entrepreneur. It lands about his face and neck. (The narrator can't even believe this shit.)

NINA (hacking then spitting) Fuck you gym shoe!

NARRATOR: The Asian spits back, Nina ducks and Jacky misses. The narrator is wondering if Jay-Jay should be watching this and what he'll allegedly steal next.

Jacky: (Spitting) Fucka Yu

NARRATOR: Nina spits again and hits the target. The ninjas separate the two and the drama ends as security approaches. Jay Jay is jumping up and down with excitement because he gets to keep the stolen ball.

Narrator (to Nina): Why did you get so upset by Jacky accusing your son of stealing if your son was innocent?

CONTINUED ON NEXT PAGE

KUNG-FU FIGHTING (cont.)

Nina (with attitude):
First of all, he woke me up out of my sleep!

Narrator (thinking - bitch why the fuck you sleepin at work in the first damn place – but says...): At work?

Narrator: Nina and the ninjas were all dumbfounded by what they all thought was a rhetorical and stupid ass question. Nina was more upset with dude waking her up at work than her son being accused of stealing. Simply fabulous.

The (Drama Never) End(s).

Just when I thought ish couldn't get any worse, it did. Nina went out and bought a taser. By the next month she had tased more ninjas then Miami-Dade Police Department. Be that as it may, I still felt sorry for her after she reached in her pocket to pull out a cigarette and accidentally tased herself in front of me. She was shakin' like a saltshaker.

THE
G
THANG

If you discover your child is gay, they're still your kid. Love, respect, and protect them. Many people will be waiting for them to crash and burn. Your child's got S.O.U.L. A Spirit Of Unconventional Love (S.O.U.L.)

Being gay is not a lifestyle choice. Living gay is. Living a lie is always an option, but why should you have to.

Spiritually speaking, God doesn't have to forgive your child because God does not condemn. Don't allow religion to kill your child's S.O.U.L. You don't want your child to ever consider suicide as an option.

So be sure and tell your children you accept them for who they are and also tell them....

God Accepts You

TALKIN' WHITE

Hood parents, if you don't learn and speak standard English you and your children will go out and make fools of yourselves on interviews and as an eye witnesses on the evening news. The only way you learn anything is by practicing. The same is true for learning English.

I was fortunate. My parents spoke English. We tend to talk and sound a lot like our parents unless we make an effort not to.

If yo mama says strimp, scrimps or swimps there's a good chance you can't say shrimp. We have a tendency of droppin the endins off our words.

Don't do it in yo interviews or at work. It makes you appear uneducated. Fool the people. Don't keep it real on your interviews. My best advice is use teachers and professionals who can speak English to help you out. However, you have to be careful because some teachers break verbs unconsciously.

Seen and saw are two of the most commonly misused verbs many people use everyday that could keep them from getting the job. It's important to know when to turn it on and off.

Here's an example:

> *I seen that in the news.*

> NEVER use "seen" without a helping verb such as "have or had." The correct way to say this sentence is:

> *I saw that in the news.*

> If you want to say "seen," the correct way to use it in a sentence is:

> *I have seen that already.*

PARENTHOOD VS. HOOD PARENT

So until you get all the "I seens" out of your system go with "I saw" and remember to practice using standard English or what some call "talkin' white" e'rr day.

Reading books, magazines, newspapers, listening to news anchors, reporters and talk show hosts and practicing by speaking it are some of the best ways to learn the King's English.

THE
DIRT

PARENTHOOD VS. HOOD PARENT

Hood parents, I want to talk to you about soap, water, deodorant and lotion. Children ain't supposed to be musty, and dirty with too little clothes and nappy ass hair. You shouldn't be out and about with them at the mall, flea market or Pay Day Loans flaunting your neglect. This is *wretched*[57].

Their necks, elbows, feet and knees should be the same color as the rest of their body. Teeth should be brushed regularly, at least twice a day, not just on special occasions. You don't want ninjas at school taking the "L" out of your darling little Ashley's name. Introduce your kids to lotion AFTER they bathe. Dirt and lotion is not a good look.

Chances are yo' mama was hood and proud of it. You would seem to be the likely candidate to make change happen.

If a child tells you they took a bath yesterday remind them that they ate yesterday, too. If your child needs some TLC hand him a bar of Caress. If your daughter asks you what are you going to leave her in your will, Lever 2000. When the kids ask you what's for dessert tell them a Dove bar. If they scream, "Yeah, an ice cream bar!" Tell them, "no, bar soap!" Kids tend to act like they're mad at soap and water. Like soap beat 'em up and water stole their bike. Remind them their butt is ebony the soap is Ivory add some water and you got perfect harmony.

In the words and voice of Richard Pryor,

"You got to wash yo' ass."

---

57   *Fucked up*

99 BOTTLES

PARENTHOOD VS. HOOD PARENT

Don't put cereal in your baby's bottles unless a physician prescribes it. It's ghetto, triflin' and lazy. Nurse Practitioner Caroll-Perry suggests feeding your baby with a baby spoon if they're old enough to eat cereal. This may be why your baby is congested and has difficulty breathing.

If you're drug and alcohol free consider breastfeeding. This is the primary reason you have lovely lady lumps, not to discount the secondary reason. I know your milkshake brings all the boys to the yard.

NAME CHANGE

PARENTHOOD VS. HOOD PARENT

There's an old saying that big mama used to say, "What the fuck they name that baby that shit for? That's a Muthin-fuckin' shame." We knew what she meant.

If we avoid the top 5 mistakes most hood parents make when naming their children we'll be good. The names need to be changed to protect the innocent.

kool rules

Rule #1

The letter *Q* or the *Q* sound can no longer be used in any name whatsoever. Fuck *Q*.

Rule #2

No more father / mother combinations. For instance:

Mother's name:	Tiffany
Father's name:	Cliff
Child's name:	Cliffany

This ain't pretty; it's pretty-ugly and Ghet - toe.

Rule #3

No more names beginning with La or ending in sha or eisha or anything that makes the sha sounds. African names with meaning are not included. Why give employers a heads up that you're child is a ninja?

Rule #4

Instead of pulling names out of your anus you must use books with baby names to choose from. Names should have true meaning.

Rule #5

Drinking and driving is illegal. Now naming babies after drinks and cars are prohibited, too. A 60 year old Mercedes and her girlfriend Tequila driving around in a Neon drunk off Brandy is not a good look.

The names are getting so bad now it kinda makes black folk wish they were *Caublasian*.[58]

---

58   *Tiger Woods self-proclaimed race so he won't have to be associated with the ninjas.*

**8
DAYS
A WEEK**

8 DAYS A WEEK

You got good cops and bad cops. Good teachers and bad teachers. You got good parents and you got Brittney Bitch.

Look, everybody is not cut out for parenting that's why God made hysterectomies, tubal ligations, vasectomies, birth control, nannies, adoption, abortion, Child Protective Service (CPS) and *Lorena Bobbitt*.[59]

Parenting is harder than Hugh Heffner. Parenting is not a full time job. Full time jobs are typically 40 hours a week.

Real parenting is 25 hours a day, 8 days a week, and 369 days a year plus overtime. Once the child reaches 21 or so, then you go on-call for life. You parent as long as you live and 6 years after you're dead. It takes a while for the kids to stop calling. "Mama!"

"I'm dead bitch."

If your children are blessed with super cool grandparents and cool aunts and uncles you are fortunate. Some parents have no extended family to count on.

If you don't have a support system in place before you have children, don't have children. It's too much to bare alone. The next thing you know you're trying to drown your children and frame a black man in a ski mask

---

59   *A woman who cut off her husband's penis and threw it out the window.*

CABLE FREE

CABLE FREE

When I asked Tre, a 5th grader, why he curses so much and where he learned such foul language, he said, "TV. I watch a lot of movies."

Some of the most effective parents have learned how to raise their children without TV. Don't throw the book to the window to the wall. I know TV is what we do in America, but it's having a negative impact on your children. I know you see it.

Your son wouldn't think to put a tattoo on his neck, face or hand, or rock an iced-out grill if it wasn't for the ~~not so~~ wonderful world of rap videos.

Your daughter wouldn't be ghetto fabulous and a shone if it were not for the wonderful world of dirty, sexy cable. She would just be fabulous.

The bad part is your kids think or act like these mental ass ideas are their own. They are plugged into the hood matrix. Unplug their asses.

I also know TV is a great baby sitter. But you must weigh your options. If you're not monitoring what your children watch you will regret it after it's too late.

My mother was born and raised in the south. She saw her first TV at fifteen. As a result, she graduated from high school in Milwaukee, WI in 1952 when she was 16 years old. Reading, writing, creating and engaging with her family was her pastime when she wasn't picking cotton in Mississippi.

Monitor the number of hours your children watch TV or sit at the computer on Myspace and Facebook. Then you will have your answer to why they can't pass the standardized tests in school. They got an A in Twitter and an F in Science. Now you're ready to do some physical education.

PARENTHOOD VS. HOOD PARENT

TV can be poisoning, persuasive, and pathetic, or it can be educational, entertaining and enlightening. You have the power to influence your children just like the TV and you do so consciously or unconsciously everyday.

The TV is twisted. Rarely will you see animals being harmed or killed on film or a TV series. You won't find animal abuse in a movie for entertainment purposes because the general public and PETA doesn't want to see animals being harmed. We love animals. Human beings? Not so much.

Now if you want to see a girl or woman being raped, ravished, pillaged and plundered on TV or in a film, not a problem. Since men control mass media, seldom will you see men being raped on TV or film. The rapes in prison get no airtime and is rarely investigated or discussed. It makes men too uncomfortable. Besides, nobody cares to know because "real" men don't get raped. Gay dudes get raped and they should like it so it's whatever. Since it's gay, we rather not even discuss it. It's shameful.

Heterosexual rape? It's a shame when you don't get it on tape. So Hollywood produces movies that show women being sexually violated on a regular.

Do you want to see mortal combat, humans tortured and killed? Not a problem. Just turn on the TV or go to a movie. Killing kids? No problem. Killing a kid goat? Big problem. Never. The animal rights activist will be all over it. Kill a person. People pay to see it. Dog fight = jail time, ask Mike Vick. Humans fight = time to get paid. It's called prize fighting, a billion dollar industry. If it don't make dollars it don't make $ense.

Is Art imitating life or vice versa?

My mother was a divorcee with four kids. She had to work and complete her college degrees simultaneously. She's quick to tell you the television helped raise me. But that was a long time ago.

CABLE FREE

There was only so much damage that Ironside, Mannix, Get Trixie Love, Speed Racer, The Munsters, The Courtship of Eddie's Father, Charlie's Angels, the Mickey Mouse Club (in black & white), Barnaby Jones, The Man from Atlantis, Fantasy Island, the Love Boat, Lost in Space, Gilligan's Island and the ABC After School Specials were going to do to my psyche.

The most risqué thing on TV back then was Electric Company. I think Easy Reader, played by Morgan Freeman, was pimpish. But he liked to read. I'm pretty sure he liked to puff, too. He was too cool. He had to be *putting something in the air*.[60]

Now if television is raising your children today your children are in serious danger. Sex, scandal, murder, mayhem, violence, crime and that's just the 6 O'clock news.

When I was about 13, I remember reading a poster on my cousin Ben's bedroom wall and it stuck. It read...

If you can't Baffle them with Brilliance

Befuddle them with Bullshit.

A television executive must have come up with this shit. This is the hidden message behind the majority of what you find on TV. You and your children spend so much valuable time in front of the TV, you've become human robots.

Children have become so desensitized and numb to murder that they *LOL*[61] when somebody gets shot, killed, beat down on TV or on the corner.

Are parents allowing their children to major in gang banging in middle school? Is it the TV that glorifies violence? Is it the bad

---

60 *Smoking herbal essence*
61 laugh out loud

PARENTHOOD VS. HOOD PARENT

news that comes on daily via the local news that is aiding and abetting the violence in the community?

I had to give this some thought. I never had a desire to rob a bank until I was sitting home one night watching the 11 o'clock news and saw a dude get away with robbing a bank. Then I thought, yeah that's a good idea. I ain't got no money either. Then I remembered I didn't have a getaway car. Dayum!

Then the next night on the news I saw a dude steal a car at gunpoint in a parking lot. It was caught on tape. I hadn't thought about grand theft auto before. I practiced on the video game so mentally I was ready. Cool, I thought, I'll just steal my getaway car.

Then I was sitting there thinking dayum to myself. I don't have a gat what was I going to do? Just my luck the next night on the news I saw a pair of 13-year-old twin bothers in Indiana rob a gun store. Before they robbed the gun store they had stolen a car, too, so I knew I was on the right track and I had the local news to thank for broadcasting it over and over again. Otherwise, I would have been clueless.

I soon realized the news is at least 50 percent responsible for a lot of the madness we see. Parents get credit for the other 50 percent. Why? If the news didn't show it, we wouldn't see it 24/7.

When they get done with the murder and mayhem in your city on the north, south, east and west sides and surrounding suburbs, then they take you to the tragedy, despair, and crime in the suburbs then after that they take you on a trip around the world for more devastation.

Companies pay billions of dollars a year for advertising. If you commit the right crime you can go to jail and make a name for yourself. The news is free advertising. Free press. Some folk just want 15 minutes of fame. Others want infamy.

Why do you think people are hiding dead bodies in dumpsters? The news! I never thought about putting my dead bodies in a dumpster until I saw it on the news. Before the news we were just leaving bodies at the crime scene. They will run the intro over and over again. A SIXTEEN YEAR OLD GIRL WAS FOUND DEAD IN A DUMBSTER next at 11. Don't let it be a blond girl with blue eyes. Then the story creates a life of its own. The world runs to tune in and watch and for what?

I don't get it. How is this information adding to your peaceful existence? It's not. All it does is educate would-be criminals as to where to hide dead bodies, good banks to rob and who shot who. Thanks for the tip and to the TV crime shows that teach you how to commit the perfect murder.

It's the same logic slave masters used. They didn't want Negroes to read because they wanted them to remain ignorant. If I was an enslaved African and I read in the Freedom Journal that there were slave revolts jumpin' off, then I would eventually revolt, too. "Oh we fighting for freedom? That's wassup! We'll burn down our massa's crib, too." This information in the Freedom Journal happened to be good and helpful news, but it works the same way with bad news.

The news also strengthens stereotypes. I was never afraid of black people on the street until I began watching the news. This is why white woman automatically become aware of their pocketbook when they see me coming. Shit…I'm scared of me.

The majority of white men are not serial killers, the majority of Latino men are not rapists and the majority of black men are not involved in gang related activities. All Native Americans are not alcoholics and own casinos. All Asians don't own beauty supply stores. And all Arabs don't own gas stations and corner stores. I could be wrong about the last two, but I'm trying to prove a point.

PARENTHOOD VS. HOOD PARENT

We have a way of accentuating the negative and overlooking the positive in this country and on the news. No wonder we are the country with the highest murder and violent crime rate. We advertise it for free.

People are not that wild about good news or the news would be showing it. We want to hear about the crime drama. Admit it. We love bad news.

Guess who got shot? Guess who's in jail? Guess who's dead? Guess who's missing? Guess who's pregnant again? Damn! There comes a time in life when you have to start asking, "What's good?"

I'm not mad at the witch from The Wiz for singing, "Don't nobody bring me no bad news!" I live by this. But often times people may think you are inconsiderate or not compassionate if you're not interested in the daily and routine drama that goes on in the hood. I say, call it what you will.

How can we get the ignorant to take a giant leap forward? Gandhi, Buddha, and King said we must do it through NONviolence. Are we wiser than them? Or did the Crips, the Bloods, the east coast / west coast rappers and Hitler get it right?

Parents teach your children to think outside the bun and use their powers for good. The status quo is at minimum ~ fucked up.

THE PRO-JECTS

PARENTHOOD VS. HOOD PARENT

So what you're straight out of Compton, Crown Heights, or the West side of Chicago. Just because you may have been born and raised in low-income housing or a tenement does that mean you have to die there?

You can achieve fame and fortune like Venus and Serena. You could even settle for greatness. How about that?

Yeah I've been to the "Poke & Beans" in Miami and the The Taylor Homes, State Way Gardens, the Ickies and Cabrini Green in Chicago. And do you know what I see?

I see greatness. I see greatness not living up to its full potential. I see apathy, too.

The world may be a ghetto in pockets. But the earth is rich. When and if you discover peace on earth during this birth time, then you will experience bliss on earth as well.

I know the streets raised you and you are true to the *game*[62], but if you decide to parent, not just have kids, but *P.A.R.E.N.T.*[63] then you will need to love and protect your children more than you love the streets. You do that by making sure that they get educated and not educated by the streets alone. Because they will need money to get out the hood in order to reach back and help free the minds of "the Others."

When "snitches get stitches" is valued more than education, L.A, CHI, NYC, DC, ATL, MIA, Philly, and Houston - we got a problem. Philly used to be known as the city of brotherly love. Now, because of the murder rate and ninjas, Philadelphia is known as Killahdelphia. That's wretched.

---

62   *One who was raised by the streets and will remains a hustler 'til they die*

63   *Defined in upcoming section*

THE PRO-JECTS

I know what you sayin' and I hear you. "I'M SO HOOD!" You wear yo pants below yo' waist, you're tatted up, you're sportin' *gold fronts*,[64] and your chain hangs low. The hood life. Dudes at Morehouse must be *hatin'*[65].

I know most kats don't want to be free from the streets. It's all they know. But the bruthas that do want something different and want more out of life, more power to you.

You aint turning your back on the hood by getting out. You're gettin' your higher ed on not just getting high. Then coming back and creating change from the inside out. You teach by example. You the shit, man! That's wassup. Studies show "quick cash" leads to slow jail time quick, fast and in a hurry.

Don't forget urban renewal is equivalent to Negroid removal. They're gettin' and got rid of y'all. Many of the Projects are sitting on prime real estate. Cabrini Green (Where J.J. and the Good Times crew cribbed) – 7 minutes north of the Magnificent Mile in downtown Chicago by Oprah's crib - is now black history, along with the Robert Taylor Homes, and many other projects.

So since you're getting relocated anyway to places where it's real hard to be real hard without being locked up and you know they won't let you out, you should strive for goodness and grace for your children's and God's sake.

---

64   *gold teeth aka grill*
65   *jealous hatred*

THE RAP GAME
(Rated P for Pathetic)

THE RAP GAME

This section is all about rap music - aka hippity hop - which falls under freedom of speech so I will use freedom of speech to discuss the politics of rap, including where its been, where it is and where it's going. Parental involvement is advised.

When you hear bullshit rap songs you are bound to say, "That's the dumbest shit I have ever heard."

The dumbest shit I ever heard in a rap song is, "I ain't friendly." And "Real niggahs don't speak." This is some of the most ignent shit infecting black folk today. It's being passed on through rap, hip-hop, and now the black community like a shone on spring break.

I hear teenage children repeating this bullshit like it's a law. "I ain't friendly." I guess teachers, parents and grandparents don't have it hard enough. We don't need ignorant ass rap lyrics to make our jobs even harder.

What we need is peace and understanding in the schools and at home and this ca-Rap ain't helping.

This pisses me off because I like rap. I'm from the hip hop generation. But this shit? These rappers are *blowin' me*.[66] Being friendly today means you're soft and weak. This must mean being "unfriendly" is hard and wassup. This is some lame ass shit. Real niggahs may not speak, but REAL BRUTHAS DO SPEAK.

The rap game is getting harder and harder and weaker and weaker at the same time from the record labels to the artists' names, to songs and album titles. Everything must be hard or you're considered soft. It doesn't matter whether you're male or female being soft in the rap game is not a good look.

---

66   *Pissin' me off.*

PARENTHOOD VS. HOOD PARENT

Back in the day, rappers rapped about *SELF-DESTRUCTION*. They were putting the black community on notice by letting us know we were headed for self-destruction. It was one the most lyrically conscious rap songs of all time, but we missed the message.

Of course it never got the Grammy.

I believe *It's Hard Out Here for a Pimp*, from the *Hustle & Flow* soundtrack walked away with the little golden statue, though. Insanity.

Whitney Houston didn't even get an Oscar for *I Will Always Love You* and the Bodyguard soundtrack was the best-selling movie soundtrack of all time.

I want to take time out to thank the academy for blowing smoke up my ass. Now we know what the academy recognizes as real music. Or are they just making sure Negroes in the community continue to strive for pimpdumb?[67]

Back in the 80s rappers were serious, yet cool. Kool Mo D, Run DMC, Curtis Blow, MC Lyte, Queen Latifah, Public Enemy, Heavy D, Yo Yo. We had great rappers, but they just weren't hard enough. They had no gun charges, they weren't criminal minded, and they weren't caught up with shooting and killing each other. There was no East Coast / West Coast beef. The only time we heard about beef was when that Wendy's commercial came on and John McCain while in drag asked, "Where's the Beef?"

---

67   *Dumb ass pimps*

FEMALE MCs

PARENTHOOD VS. HOOD PARENT

Fast forward 20 years and we have gone from Queen Latifah putting Ladies First to the Queen Bitch (Lil' Kim) who prides herself on *drinking babies*.[68] Also, if you give her what she needs you can "fuck her 'til she bleeds." Sounds red hot if you like "ketchup on your fries." And if you give her the keys to the jeep, she'll even suck you to sleep. A bang for yo buck, *fo sho*.[69]

Yo Yo said, "I'm not a ho no." The Baddest Bitch, Trina, said, "I'm phat in the ass" and she wants to know do you want to taste. And according to her she "fucks like a porn star." Impressive resume, no? Yeah, no.

You don't need ice cream if you're kickin it with Khia because you can lick her neck, her back, her possy and her crack. The Flavor of the month is pubic dough. It's chunky, but funky.

My female rap queens, if you discovered you can spin around on a penis without falling off there's no need to rap about it. Get it on tape! I don't mean that. Get it on Blu-ray.

I can appreciate your possy being *off the chain*[70] but why are you rapping about it Jackie O? Dudes will discover this when they penetrate you. You want your coochie to be your claim to fame?

There has to be something else hot about you other than your sex game being tight.

Truth be told Superhead got all y'all on lock anyway so why waste time rapping about your possy. There has to be something else that you do well besides ride a nice penis. Maybe you can *throw down in the kitchen*.[71] There are a lot of words surrounding food that rhyme and you could still curse if you felt the need.

---

68   *When one swallows after performing fellatio to completion*

69   *for sure*

70   *Good as hell*

71   *To cook well*

Imagine these lyrics to the beat of that *My Neck My Back* joint.

My Breast My Thighs

*First you gotta sink yo teeth into it –
Don't stop chew it chew it
Then you grab the buns
Toss the salad before you come*

*Soul food is what I do
Just taste my barbecue
My chicken is off the chain
Makes every ninja go insane*

*My wings, my fries, lick my breast and my thighs
My wings, my fries, lick my breast and my thighs*

It still would've been a hit Khia. Monique and the big girl crew would eat this shit up! BET Awards here they come. Aretha, the queen of soul food, would've sung this at the inauguration. This is how Jill Scott blew up. You know how many big girls bought her CD. She sings about food on every damn CD. Grits, fish, chicken, long walks to KFC and shit.

Female MCs, step ya game up. You're a lyricist. You're a queen of rap. You're not *Miss Becky*[72]. Girls and young gay dudes look up to you. Can you drop knowledge instead of just rappin' about droppin' to ya knees? I thought, "Real bitches do real things," meant something much deeper.

---

72   *A female who is really good at performing fellatio.*

RAP
DUDES

In order for a dude to make it in the rap game he needs jail time, visible bullet wounds, a paper chasing mentality, and be tatted-up. He must rap about drinkin, druggin, fuckin', suckin, lickin, lappin, bumpin' humpin, and grinding.

50 Cent suggests you should get rich or die trying and Biggie professes the two most important things in life is fucking female dogs and getting money. You'll need the money to pay for all yo pups when yo bitch gets pregnant.

(In the voice of Sophia from the Color Purple)

"I loves hip-hop, God knows I do," but I'm not a 13-year-old impressionable teenager who believes the hype! Children believe in the player's anthem with all their heart and soul. This is what they aspire to become.

My 18-year-old nephew has *get rich or kill yoself* on his Myspace page. Since he has no money, no job, no car and is broker than a joke his mother had to ask him, "When's the funeral"?

This is why I wouldn't allow my dog to see American Gangster. We glorify gangsters more then we do the King of Kings. The Lord of Lords and the Great I Am.

We had Niggahs Wit Attitudes (NWA) back in the day. Now we need (NWG) Niggahs with Gratitude.

Record labels like Def Row and Murder Inc. had to eventually change their names to The Row and Inc. Records to purify their image in the eyes of the law. I guess they were too hard for their own damn good.

But that wasn't hard enough. Today we got rap groups like Three 6 Mafia, Mac 10, Junior Mafia. Juvenile. But that wasn't hard enough. So we got 2Pistols and Young Gunz.

PARENTHOOD VS. HOOD PARENT

What's next? Lil' Killyolilpunkasslikeamuthafucka?!

As a male rapper you also have to be able to rap about any violence that has been perpetrated against you that you lived to tell.

50 Cent rapped the lyrics, "I been hit with two shells…" blahzayskippywahoo-gives a damn. If this doesn't impress you, you're soft or you don't give a damn about the hype.

And if you were a part of the dope game you must rap about it. I believe its part of your contract.

Tupac rapped, "Even though I sell rocks it feels good putting money in your mailbox." Blah blah blah is all I hear. Off the record, "Dear Mama" is a hot track.

The Album titles are even harder. Titles like Biggie's "Ready to Die" and Tupac's "Life After Death" have sold millions. But where are they now?

I know women like hard legs, ruff necks, six packs and a thugs hug, but dayum. How hard do you have to be?!

Rappers are acting, ladies and gentlemen, because the image sells. Ain't nobody that damn hard. Damn wanabee Tony Montanas. I know you see it. Meanwhile, kids are trying to emulate what they see on TV - shit that ain't even real. It's make-believe boys and girls. Their job is to sell albums.

Pants saggin' showing off your anus because you think it's a trend. Why would you want dudes checking out your ass and having anal thoughts? You ain't in jail no more. It appears as though you want somebody to pop that coochie. In the words of Public Enemy #1 ~ Dudes and dudettes, Don't, don't, don't, don't believe the hype!

I'm feelin that new wave hip hop flavor that MR. CLUTCH is bringin' in his "radio ready" CD Grandma's Hand. "It's not your average make it rain, shoot 'em up bang bang type of rap."

NAUGHTY BY NURTURE

PARENTHOOD VS. HOOD PARENT

People don't shoot in the theater on Broadway. But there have been shots fired in the movie theater I went to as a shorty. The violence on the big screen was being played out right in front of my very eyes. There you have it, art imitating life or is it the other way around?

When you leave a Broadway play you're hungry for more, your heart is dancing and your voice is humming. When you leave the trap house your kids are hungry, your heart is racing and your breath is *hummin.*'[73]

There is no group of people smarter than other groups of people. Wiser? Definitely. People in Japan are excelling in technology because they don't watch 12 hours or more of TV a day. If you took your baby and set him in Japan and picked him up a few years later he'd come back speaking Japanese and building computers and cell phones and shit. If you leave him in the hood and pick him up a few years later his pants are saggin down to his knees, he's tatted up, he's speaking some language you don't understand and his main goals are money, cars, clothes and hoes. To a fool this sounds good.

Sociologists call it nature vs. nurture. Dr. Kunjufu calls it a conspiracy to destroy black boys. I call it Parenthood vs. Hood Parent. Outside influences can negatively impact your children. More than likely society got to you first. So now you and society are double-teaming your shorties.

Your surroundings impact your life. If you want to come out of poverty, even at a late stage in life, stop doing what people in poverty do. You are what you think you are and you are what you think.

---

[73]   *To have bad breath aka Kickin' like Jackie Chan*

President Barack Obama is helping this world make the transition from race matters to human matters. The truth is without Bush there could be no Obama. Bush pushed us to one end - the bottom - and now President Obama is taking us spiritually higher. It takes a certain level of confidence to believe you can do anything. Swim, steal, ride a bike, parent or become president.

People did not vote for President Obama because he's black. Well some did, and some whites voted for McCain because he's not black. But on a whole, President Obama won votes because minds and spirits can communicate truth through vibrations and frequencies as well as with the aid of the spoken word.

You can and you do communicate messages every minute of every day to your children. Spoken and unspoken and by smokin' and not smoking. Some parents treat plants and animals better than their children. Show love to every living thing and being.

THE SWEETEST TATTOO

THE SWEETEST TATTOO

Even the sweetest tattoo has to be in the right place. I'm a firm believer in to each his own and to each her own. But when it comes to tattoos lil mama, you have to ask yourself whether you really want to rock a pair of paws on your breast when you're 82.

Paws on your 82-year-old breasts are not a good look, ma. Truth be told it's not a good look at 22. I mean it's ghetto fabulous but when you leave the ghetto the fabulous doesn't go with you.

First of all gravity is a bitch. The paws that once sat on your cleavage will now be positioned somewhere around your navel. Your new bra size is 44 Long and your paws look like they might have arthritis.

Ladies and Gentlemen, you are pushing it to the limit in a bad way. Remember, less is more. Think about your professional career or lack thereof while in high school then you will make better judgments on where to put your discreet tattoo.

You haven't got the job at the record label, yet. You haven't signed a multi-million dollar contract with any sports team so what's really going on mami and papi? Is your judgment really that fucked up? Does what you see on TV really mean the world to you?

Your ideas are not your own. You copy what you see. If you change the channel -meaning your focus - you can see a whole new world. "There's a different world than where you came from."

DRINKIN' & DRUGGIN'

Please don't drink, drug and parent simultaneously. You don't want this to be your claim to fame. There are dry drunks who no longer drink, but are not sober in Spirit. There are people who drink sociably who are sober-minded.

This might sound crazy, but if you're going to abuse drugs and alcohol why don't you put off having kids until you get out of recovery and have been clean for several years. This way you won't impart your misery, depression and dysfunction on innocent children. Deal or No Deal?

If you discovered you were an addict after you had children, well yes, your kids love you drunk and all and you love them, too. But what's love got to do with it? You also love crack, *yak*[74] and that monkey on your back.

So realize your children will love and respect you more clean and sober more than slick and greasy. You don't have to hit rock bottom before you get up and you don't have to hit rocks.

If you happen to develop a habit after you have children this is what immediate family, extended family and foster care is for. Yes, you may need the child support or government check your children are bringing in to support your habit and that's ~~not~~ understandable, but what's more important ~ Your kids' well-being and peace of mind or a piece of crack? Don't answer that, it's a rhetorical question.

This may be a difficult decision to make, but who's going to parent your kids while you're in the streets, locked in your bedroom or bathroom bingeing or at the trap house?

Drug counselors say it's important to love your kids more than you love drinking and drugging.

I guess you could call it a sacrifice, but it's really a win-win situation. Your children's win is you save them from a childhood

---

74   *Abbreviation for Cognac*

of hell. Your win is you get to drink, smoke and cuss for the rest of your life or until you go get clean. And your beautiful children won't be forced to raise themselves or have visual images of you liquored and doped up embedded in their memory bank for the rest of their hot damn life.

You can love your kids from a distance or use birth control until you get the help you need. Your conscious and your children will thank you in the beginning, middle and end.

HI-Q

PARENTHOOD VS. HOOD PARENT

My papacito taught me, "Don't pick up anything you can't put down." Hood parents tell their children, "Don't blow my high." It does not take a blunt in the morning or afternoon, depending on when you wake up, to get your day started. This is called addiction. A vice is a vice is a vice whether it be coffee, food, cocaine, etc.

Moderation is the shit.

Some of you are smoking away your brain cells when you need above average intelligence in order to properly raise children.

Only 1% of the population has an IQ over 135. They are no doubt part of the same 1% that is running the country. On the other end of the scale roughly 5% of the population has an IQ under 70. This is the benchmark of cognitive disabilities or mental retardation. People with such low IQs are no doubt responsible for inventing road rage. Although you may have never had your IQ tested, where do you honestly think you fit in?

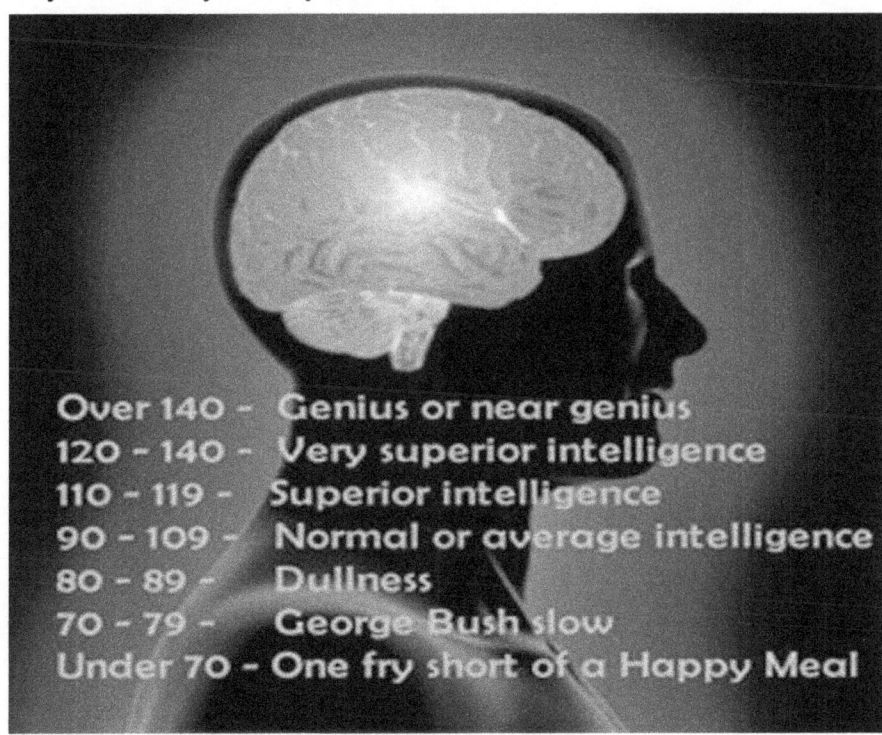

Over 140 - Genius or near genius
120 - 140 - Very superior intelligence
110 - 119 - Superior intelligence
90 - 109 - Normal or average intelligence
80 - 89 - Dullness
70 - 79 - George Bush slow
Under 70 - One fry short of a Happy Meal

On the parenting tip, y'all know it's some double-digit mugs out there raising kids. If you don't have a triple digit IQ and or if you're not a two-process thinker you probably shouldn't be making babies just yet. Dull people often produce dull kids.

The most important thing to learn from this is the majority of the people can raise their level of intelligence through reading and traveling outside the neighborhood where they grew up.

There are people in Chicago who have never left the west side to go downtown or to the north side. I love my homies in Chicago, but God loves the truth. The difference between a gifted child and a non-gifted child is life experiences.

DRIVER'S HEAT

I'm not sure if anyone noticed, but there are many children walking around with anger and hostility. There are also many adults and parents walking around mad as hell for no apparent reason. Mad parents produce angry kids and kids with attitudes.

Walk around any hood and you will find anger is the culture. People walk around looking mad for no apparent reason. It's cool to be mad.

You can choose the attitude that you want to embrace everyday of your life. No one can make you hit them. I'm not referring to self-defense, of course.

Thanks to road rage we have drivers who say fuck you to other drivers like it's a salutation. Congratulations Miami for winning the title of the city with the #1 Road Rage in America.

Your rage is learned behavior. It's all ego based and the ego looks for shit to attack. Your children look for behavior to mimic so when you get behind the wheel don't go into attack mode. Driving is like sex if you're not safe you can die.

Yes, you need to be a defensive driver, but not a defensive nut behind the wheel. There are hundreds of cars in front of you at any given time so there is no need to trip when one car gets in front of you.

Your aggressive behavior is not you.

You have to practice being peaceful if you don't want drama in your life.

Many children and adults want and need a warm loving hug everyday and since they are not getting it, the lack of love turns into aggression and that begins to feel so good to your ego that you can't get enough. As a result you forget about authentic love and settle for pain and drama.

PARENTHOOD VS. HOOD PARENT

Your kids are no doubt riding shotgun so remember to show love when you are in the driver's seat. Don't just use your memory to remember bullshit. You can R.I.P. while you're still alive.

Turn the page, raise your right hand and read The BENN Commandments aloud:

THE BENN

I don't own the road, highway, or the lane I'm driving in ~ the city does.

I will use my damn signal when I'm changing lanes as a courtesy to other drivers and to avoid accidents

I will not accelerate like an asshole when I see someone signaling to change lanes to get in front of me. I'm smarter than a 5th grader

I will not drive 55 in the passing lane (far left lane on the highway). I will stay my ass to the right

I will not slow down on the street or highway to gape, gaze or gawk at an accident or someone changing a freakin' tire. This could cause another accident and delay traffic. I will watch the news when I take my ass home if I wish to see murder and mayhem

COMMANDMENTS

THE BENN

I will not curse out other drivers on the road because it's rude and ignorant. Although it makes my ego feel good as hell ~ I look dumb as hell.

Since I do dumb shit when I'm driving, I will excuse other drivers when they do dumb shit, and I will not blow at them or curse them like I'm a fuckin' nut.

I understand it's my fault I'm running late not the people on the road. I could have crawled my ass out of bed earlier. I can kick my own ass and accept what is.

I will dispatch my angels every time I get in the car to keep me safe from harm and to keep me present. This will help me to avoid accidents and speeding tickets. It will also keep me at peace behind the wheel.

When I'm stuck in traffic, I will exhale and tell myself, "I am where I'm supposed to be." I'm fortunate my whip is not overturned and blazing in a nearby ditch.

COMMANDMENTS

MENTAL WEALTH

PARENTHOOD VS. HOOD PARENT

While working for Miami-Dade Public Schools, I had the opportunity to work with teen parents and pregnant teens at an alternative high school.

Every last one of the teen parents I spoke to said they did not like counseling. Some had been raped repeatedly, sold their bodies for cash, had numerous STDs, abused sexually by a biological parent, had parents who were killed in front of them, or had parents doin' jail time.

Some had baby daddies who physically, verbally, and emotionally abused them, but it was OK and soon forgiven because he was phyne. Many parents of the teen parents were also guilty of verbal and physical abuse.

I would ask the teen parents who had experienced trauma in their lives, "Have you tried counseling to help you heal?" The responses, "I tried it. I didn't like it." "She was too nosy." "He was always asking too many questions." "She keep asking me how I feel" and my favorite, "He talk too slow for me."

HOOD PARENTS:

"THERE'S STRENGTH IN NUMBERS,

DO NOT UNITE!"

The less economically advantaged (po folk) can't afford to hire people (nannies) to raise their children. Joan Rivers reminds her daughter on a regular basis how many times she had to get out of bed in the middle of the night, walk to the top of the staircase and scream for the governess, then crawl back in bed.

But what are the children of low-income families to do? There is no super nanny at their disposal.

Now don't get it twisted. Rich folk abuse and neglect their children, too. See Mommy Dearest, or better yet, read the book. But there's

MENTAL WEALTH

always a way out when you got the cash, its called counseling ~ the road to recovery.

Hood parents, though, don't like counseling. Oh Hell 2 the NO! They think counseling is for punks. They think something must be seriously wrong with you if you go see a therapist. It's something seriously wrong with you if you don't know that there's something seriously wrong with you and you need a therapist. Da Nile is not just a river in Egypt.

After several years, dysfunction can appear to be normal if that's all you know.

You got to watch your kids and monitor them. I would've never raise a monster like Jeffrey Dahmer and not know I got a nut job for a son. As soon as my little 8 year old killed his first rabbit with his bare hands, I would have known that lil Jeffy was out of his rabbit ass mind. Jeffery would have awakened the next morning sporting a straight jacket in the county hospital's, psych ward.

I would still love my son but I would love him through a plate glass window once or twice a year for the rest of his life. You have to pay close attention to your kids, especially if they are touched.

It helps if you know if mental illness is a branch on the old family tree. The Menendez brothers, who killed their parents, never would've been me. Crazy don't just appear out of thin air. Crazy marinates over time. Parents you have to get some *withedness*[75] otherwise you will wake up one morning and you're dead.

Now Dahmer and the Menedez brothers are the extreme cases of children who may have been touched at birth. But for the most part the majority of children born into this world are innocent and precious. Then the ills of the world encumber them and take over. It is your job to remain sane and keep your children sane.

---

75   *Being aware of what your children are doing at all times*

PARENTHOOD VS. HOOD PARENT

Life is easy. People sometimes make it hard. They see everything as happening to them. They have the weight of world on their shoulders. Until you unlearn what you have been taught and relearn something new you will always feel burdened.

Remember the song you learned in preschool?

Row, Row, Row Your Boat

This song is a metaphor for life. You are the boat. You choose the path or direction that you will go in.

Gently up the stream...

There's strength in gentleness. The ego cleverly disguises itself as pimpish, crazy, loud, ghetto fabulous, ABW, etc. just to make life hard for you. Don't go with the hustle and flow just go with the flow.

Merrily, merrily, merrily, merrily...

Joy, peace, happiness, and abundance are emotions you can take with you wherever you go in life. Work, home, school, court and piss tests don't have to create anxiety any longer. Dust your shoulders off or get counseling.

If you're not at peace your ego has you trapped in thought. Stop consuming your life with the past and what you don't have. Focus on what you do have; health, life, and strength. Peace of mind is priceless; gain it and retain it. It's true, misery does love company, but nobody wants you when you're down and out.

Life is but a dream...

After people come into this world and leave this world -was their life but a dream? Are memories like dreams? Do your dreams feel real when you are asleep? When you awaken has a new dream begun? It really is miraculous when you think about the fact that an Intelligence can keep our bodies alive while we are sleeping.

When you're dreaming you become the observer of the dream. This is the same function you should maintain when you are "awake". This is the road to peace. You don't trip when shit happens. You watch life as it unfolds. For all we know we are awake when we're sleep and dreaming when we're awake. They both feel real while they are happening.

Deja vu ~ Did I dream this?

The most important thing I learned while learning Spanish is the language makes more sense than English. In English the languages causes us to attach ourselves to emotions.

For example,

I am hungry.

We are not hunger. We have hunger. That's how it is described in Spanish.

In Spanish you would say:

Tengo hambre – I have hunger.

What you can learn from this is don't attach the way you may be feeling to what or who you are. If you are as God made you then you are only love. Anything else you exhibit is not you. Anger, resentment, jealously etc. is of the ego. Put it to sleep.

We see in color and we dream in color. How fly is that? You are the dream maker whether you're sleeping or awake. So make your dreams come true.

SHAKE & BREAK

I doubt very seriously if your Grandma-nana's famous last words were, "You gots to beat yo kids." Unless your last name is Slavemaster, chill for a minute and let's try and come up with a different approach.

If you think about it your shorties weren't born with a label that says, "Beat they ass like they stole something." If this were the secret to success your children would have more than GEDs and player hatin' degrees. They would have MDs, JDs, and PhDs.

So if knocking your kids around and cussin' them the fuck out is what you do ~ may God bless 'em.

The general public calls it verbal and physical abuse. Remember "Penny" from Good Times? Her birth mama was tearing that ass up. You're doing the same thing minus the iron. Abuse is abuse. Don't shoot the author.

The reason why you shouldn't call your daughter a stupid ass bitch is because she'll believe you. You can't expect a stupid ass bitch to achieve greatness in her life or become a super star. Expect her to allow men to call her a stupid ass bitch and spend the rest of her life answering to such names. Chances are somebody referred to you as a dumb bitch and apparently you want to create another one. You're on your way.

Don't call your son a dumb ass muthafucka and then expect him to be successful in life. Your kids will believe what ever you have them believe. When your kids spread their wings they gon' fall off. How can or will they learn to fly with broken wings?

I believe they can fly. I also believe you can improve your parenting skills starting today. Teach your kids right from wrong without killing their character, confidence and creativity.

If you always do what you always did you'll always get what you always got. Many parents want their children to be the next Barack,

Donald, Oprah, Bill Gates, Hillary or Michael Jordan, Jackson, or Tyson.

However, you routinely talk to your children like they just stepped on your pinky toe. Bunions or not, that ain't right.

You've all been to a restaurant, movie theater, or your local school and witnessed innocent or not so innocent children be verbally and/or physically abused.

Typically children who are raised in this fashion, surprisingly enough, develop aggressive and violent behaviors that follow them throughout life. Since most behaviors are learned, chances are you're only repeating what has been done to you. And the question is – Did it work? Have you reached the magnitude of success that you had envisioned for yourself or are you simply living from unemployment check to welfare check to SSI check or from paycheck to paycheck?

It's very likely that you may have good intentions gone bad. If you piss on a plant once a week instead of watering it as the directions state, then you will eventually murder your plant - death by urination. But that's just it, plants, games, cars, etc. all have directions to follow. With children it's a damn toss up. Children don't come with a manual, directions or a belt.

JUST FOR PARENTS

If children came with instructions they would probably read like this:

EASY STEP-BY-STEP PARENTING INSTRUCTIONS
READ THIS BEFORE YOUR WATER BREAKS

Step 1: Always wait 24-hours before you apply a belt, shoe, switch, extension cord, or lay hands on your child. By doing this you will NOT leave permanent physical damage, skin irritation, emotional scars, hair breakage or eye injury.

Step 2: Do a simple test first to make sure your child can hear you. ☠**WARNING**☠ DO NOT say "Bitch/Muhfucka, do you hear me talking to yo ass!"

THIS MAY CAUSE SELF-ESTEEM DAMAGE!

Ask the child do they want a new cell phone, McDonald's or cash. The hearing test is complete once they respond. Now that you know they can hear you and you have their attention, DO NOT SCREAM or YELL. Use a moderate, but slightly deranged tone. Just ask them to come have a seat across from you at the table. If you can't reach them you are less likely to slap the shit out of them when they open up their mouth to lie. This will be scary enough for the child mainly because you've never done it before so they may really think you're losing your mind. Use this to your advantage. (Open and close your fists and exhale as needed to help you relax).

1. CONVERSE WITH YOUR CRUMB-SNATCHERS

Some children have a devil-may-care attitude. Some parents have a "you will do what the hell I say or I'm gon beat yo muthafuckin ass" attitude. If your children fail to follow directions you should talk TO them without screaming. Children have become used to your yelling, screaming, ranting and raving. They believe you are screaming because you have lost control. In order to gain control, you should talk to them like you have good sense. Your voice should be slightly above a whisper whereby the child has to almost strain to hear you. Just like you have to strain to hear them when they are being checked. Remember you are the parent and you are in control. Not only will your self-control confuse them, they will now believe you've got the POWER. If you can't control yourself, you won't control your children. Most of all, this is how your children will learn to control themselves. Teach by example.

2. MEET WITH YOUR TAX DEDUCTIONS

You claim them on April 15th every year. You may find weed seeds and your seeds irritating, but you can't throw them both out. Meet with your seeds. It will help them more than it will hurt you. You just need to jot down your talking points. Have weekly or biweekly family meetings. These meeting can be anywhere from 15 minutes to an hour or longer. This not only keeps you in the driver's seat it allows you to monitor what your child is doing. Discuss education, sex, politics, friends, family, work, vacations - any and everything. Keep it relaxed and informal, but bring a notebook and pen to record important information. If meetings keep major corporations and business operations running smoothly, they damn sure can help keep your family operations running smoothly.

Have your plan for their education K – 12 and college. When and if they attempt to deviate from the plan, discuss it at the family meeting. They should know early on that they will only be dating their books until they finish high school. Your boyfriend is your books. The only girlfriend you want to meet better be named Geometry.

Friends Vetted; Mother Approved.

Make sure you know where your children are at all times or least where they're supposed to be. Not just because you are financially responsible for what ever they do. But you must know their whereabouts. If they don't want you to know where they are, where they are going or where they've been invite them to the nearby shelter or park bench. Cell phones now have low jacks. Soon you won't have this problem.

3. PUT YOUR JUVENILES ON NOTICE

If your child defies your instructions or directions or gets slick out the mouth, put them on notice the first time. This is how you avoid spontaneous combustion. Sit down and have a talk with them immediately. There should be no surprises. There should be consequences and repercussions.

Place your index finger on the temple of your child's head and say, "Mommy is feeling angry. The old me wants to knock the ish out of you. The new me wants to put you on notice. If this happens again then _____ (fill in the blank) will happen." Your children must believe you're one fry short of a Happy Meal or they will not fully respect you. You don't have to be crazy to be a good parent. It just helps if your kids think you are.

4. PROGRAM YOUR CHILDREN

Children are robots that require food, love and water. If you program your children from day one you will not have to deal with the hassle of deprogramming them and reprogramming them later. The TV and their friends will be operating from TV land. Teach them how to think for themselves and don't worry about blending in with the fools of society. If you can save some of your "get hi" money and send your child to private school that's what's up! Otherwise enroll your child in a magnet or charter school. The fewer distractions your children have in school the better. Public schools are jumpin' like a disco.

5. CAUTION

- You will be tempted to wear that ass out if the child has lied to you about something. Quickly think about a time you lied to your parent or to your child and breathe. Tell your child, "Only the truth is true." And if it don't make sense it ain't true.

- Do not drink, drug, and then parent when you are fucked up. If you are not sober, your judgment may be impaired

- Do not let your child's boyfriend or girlfriend move in with you. Number 1) your child shouldn't be dating and Number 2) their parents put them out for a reason. If they left home for a valid reason refer them to their nearest relative or shelter.

- In rare cases children may curse you, scream "I hate you!" or slam doors. Ask your child to call 911 and tell the dispatch officer they are having difficulty breathing. Gently release your hands from around the child's neck and wait for the authorities. Dare them to jump bad if they wont to.

- If you discover your child is sexually active ask him or her what type of contraceptive he or she is using and calmly tell him/her they could be infected. Never smile. Take them to the clinic immediately. It's a good idea to keep color photos of STDs posted around your house. Be sure and use these photos at family meetings.

- Never say, "I ain't gon tell you again," "This is the last time I'm gon tell you," or "Didn't I tell you?" These are signs to the juvi that you enjoy screaming and repeating yourself. Say it one time and wait for them to move, but don't wait too long. Reach for the knee or walk up on them.

With no instructions, before you know it your child is hooked on drugs, in jail (sometimes next to you) and you wonder where you went wrong. Conception.

Sometimes you can do everything right and society will get to your child and do him or her in right before your eyes. So you have to provide your child with TLC (Tender Loving Care) and LCW (love, compassion and wisdom). Juveniles need love, too.

The good news is that knowledge is power and when you know better you do better. The bad news is the truly ignorant don't read. Encourage your friends and family to follow these instructions carefully.

Children are mini yous and mini mes. If flowers can grow through concrete, then greatness can bypass generations of dumb. So just because you may not be working to your full potential it doesn't necessarily mean that your child will be a chip off the old nut.

We have generations of insanity, but we also have generations of royalty. Your child speaks English because he or she was raised in a house that spoke English. Your child is not hard wired to speak English because you do. If your child was taken at birth and adopted by a Spanish speaking family in San Juan, Puerto Rico, guess what language your very own child would speak? If you guessed Espanol, eres correcto (you're right).

Before children even learn to comprehend the language you are speaking they are watching you every step of the way from day one. And since 90 percent of communication is nonverbal it's key that you become a role model for your child before the water breaks.

So talk up to your child. Don't talk down to him or her because you feel less than. Your child(ren) are a reflection of you so if you don't like what you see don't judge it, accept it for what it is and the part you played in creating a creature that talks, looks, smells and acts a lot like you.

It's called an "act" because the behavior was learned. If you used LCW everyday of your child's life, which costs nothing, you have a very good chance of producing a very good product. Most times you will get out what you put in. If you plant tomatoes you won't get bananas.

Children are an investment. Tell your children you are "growing" educated professionals in your household and if they turn out to be less than great tell them you want your money back.

SPARE THE ROD

I LOVE CHILDREN – when they're sleeping. And I'm not the only one. Where did some of today's parenting come from? The Plantation Method? Massa Knows Best? Mommy Dearest? What?!

What's your defense for beating and slapping the shit out of your kids? "Because they yo mutha fuckin kids" is not a good defense. This may come as a surprise, but the truth is your plantation parenting skills are weak, lame, and ineffective. Oh, I forgot abusive.

I have some stats to prove it. More than 50 percent of black males are not completing high school. They can finish a pint of yak and a blunt without a problem, but high school, not so muthafuckin' much.

Some of your children would be better off if you sold them back into slavery.

The Pros:

- They would develop a strong work ethic.
- They would be watched and supervised 24/7.
- They wouldn't spend hours of valuable time in front of the TV watching that *I Love New York* mess or any spin off.
- They would kill or die to read a book.

The Cons:

- Work without pay.
- Can't Vote
- Can't look at white women (this would be a pro for black women).

PARENTHOOD VS. HOOD PARENT

Now of course the NBA would have a problem with the last bullet and of course you need to be able to Barack the Vote, but what are we doing to the children?

Everything else would be pretty much the same as today.
- No reading.
- Under fed.
- Beat for nothing.
- And treated like shit.

It's been proven baby mamas and baby daddies don't know a damn thing about discipline. Ass whuppins, yes. Discipline, no. So take notes.

Today if you caught your child playing with matches you might tap their hands or if they ran in the street you might tap the legs. And no one would probably flinch.

I learned my multiplication facts thanks to Mrs. Orr and her five rulers taped together. I was in the 3rd grade at Auer Avenue in Milwaukee. Mrs. Orr would call us up one by one. She would say the problem "3x3" we would supply the answer "9."

Now if you said the wrong answer i.e. "9x4" "uuuhhh 34" Whack! And you better not move your hand because that would mean two whacks with the rulers.

Now was this the best way to get educated? No. Did it work? Yes, we studied at night and prayed our nerves didn't get the best of us. Do kids today know their math facts? Hell to the NO! And I'm talking about high school kids.

I think slavery made whuppins big in our country. If Kunta Kente were alive today he would even say, "Dayum, y'all beatin these kids like some runaway slaves!" We slap kids across the face and pop them in the mouth like they ain't shit. Pull their hair. Fight them like thugs in the street and treat them like riff raff. Call them bitches and hoes and muthafuckas like they ain't nothin' Then send them off to school so they can get a good education. Psych!

Check it out. When you knock the shit out of your kids you're also knocking the esteem, confidence, and happiness out of them, too. That's a lot of time and energy when they could just go have a seat in the bathroom.

Fortunately, some kids do shake it off and become productive members of society, but no thanks to you. As parents, it's important to be able to identify your strengths and weaknesses. If discipline is not your strong suit let me introduce you to positive and negative reinforcement.

Now the bad news is there's a good chance that you have been positively and negatively reinforcing your child's behavior the wrong way all along. The good news is it's never too late to start over again. The pros who work with children are trained to use Positive Reinforcement. Let me break it down for you.

POSITIVE REINFORCEMENT

POSITIVE REINFORCEMENT

Positive reinforcement occurs when a particular stimulus is presented after a behavior, and the behavior increases as a result, according to Sarah Maccarelli, who wrote an article for Associated Content.com. The word positive does not mean "good" in this case, but means that something is added.

Positive reinforcement comes in many forms, including concrete reinforcers, social reinforcers, and activity reinforcers.

A concrete reinforcer is something tangible that can be seen. For example, if Lasharquanta (the 'r' is silent) does all of her homework, her mom gives her a sticker.

A social reinforcer is a gesture from another person in response to a behavior. For example, if Dehandsome (former student) slam-dunks a basketball, his friend gives him a high five.

An activity reinforcer is an opportunity to engage in a fun activity. People will do something they don't enjoy for a chance to do something that they do enjoy. For example, if Breezy cleans her room, Uncle Fabian will take her out for ice cream.

NEGATIVE REINFORCEMENT

NEGATIVE REINFORCEMENT

Negative Reinforcement is when a particular stimulus is removed after a behavior, and this causes the behavior to increase as a result. Negative in this sense does not mean "bad", but that something is subtracted or taken away.

For example, if Asha's mom is always nagging her to wash the dishes (nagging is the stimulus) and when Asha does the dishes, her mom stops nagging her, then negative reinforcement has occurred. From now on, Asha is more likely to do the dishes if only to avoid her mother's nagging.

A particular behavior is strengthened by the consequence of experiencing a positive condition.

Now this is what hood parents do:

You positively reinforce bad behavior. For instance, your child curses for the first time because those are the only words he hears coming out of your mouth. Your three-year-old child says, "move bitch get out the way..." to his *project twin*[76] and because you've been drinkin and druggin all day you laugh like you at the comedy club and say, "Dat shit funnier than a muthafucka. Dat lil' niggah crazy," while you're *ROFL*.[77]

Then when you're done laughing you give him a cookie, dollar, and have him do a rap performance at family functions.

The Social Reinforcer ~ when Damani raps his uncles and aunts give him a fist pound so the behavior is bound to happen again.

The Concrete Reinforcer ~ since Damani's cussin' makes you laugh your ass off when he's done swearing you give him a cookie.

---

76   *Two children born within the same year having the same biological fathers, but different mothers.*

77   *Rolling on the floor laughing*

PARENTHOOD VS. HOOD PARENT

The Activity Reinforcer ~ if Damani remembers to go sit on the toilet instead of taking a dump in his 'draws' you allow him to perform at family functions.

Therefore you have reinforced the expected behavior concretely, socially, and actively. Now "your shawty cursing" will no doubt be strengthened and increase.

You need yo ass wupped and I say this with love.

What does this mean and what you can do if the ass whuppin' doesn't find you?

As a parent you need to be able to walk the line. If I can successfully manage a classroom with 39 eighth grade students from the south side of Chicago for six hours a day for an entire school year, then you should be able to manage however many kids you choose to have on a routine basis.

The secret, don't reward negative behavior. If your child is not following your directions don't give them anything extra and take away anything extra they have (i.e. cell phone) until they get it together. You run this, and it's OK to remind them.

P.A.R.E.N.T

PARENTHOOD VS. HOOD PARENT

The keys to having and maintaining discipline is by using the P.A.R.E.N.T. Method:
1. Patience
2. Awakening
3. Respect
4. Empower
5. Now
6. Teach by Example

P is for PATIENCE

This is a virtue most people, including parents, lack. Calling patience a virtue makes it harder for people to obtain and maintain self-control.

Many times we call something hard or challenging so we can have an excuse not to do the shit. Instead why don't we just say, "It's NEW." Because that's what it is, it's new. It's hard to the ego. But it's not hard for who you truly are; a manifestation of the Magnificent.

Therefore, your children are an incarnation of the Omnipotent as well, and the abuse will slap the innocence out of that "little son of God" in a heartbeat.

Understand this, your heartbeat, breathing and pulse are all run by an Intelligence far greater than us. You don't have to remind your heart to beat or remind yourself to breath, it just happens naturally.

It's natural that you will become more patient each day life brings, if you allow nature to take its course. Your impatience has been learned from the people around you. Go against the grain and go with the flow.

Teach your child patience by taking peace with you wherever you go. If you're calm and at peace, then you are teaching your children to be still and peaceful. Now, don't you want your child to be still? So if you're loud and ignorant, well you figure it out. The fruit doesn't fall to far from the nutty ass fruitcake.

Think wisely before you speak, remain calm. Remember you are where you are supposed to be, whether it is stuck in traffic, incarcerated, or in line at Wal-Mart with one register open. Accept it. Don't resist it. People get behind the wheel of a car and become monsters. It's insane. Relax and let it flow.

Your children will try you, no doubt. But at the end of the day you want to be able to say I raised my child with the best of my ability. You know in your heart if you're doing a half-ass job parenting. This doesn't mean you're a half-ass parent it means you need to listen to your children. If physicians still have to "practice" medicine after 12 years of college, then you can practice patience. It's a process. Woosah![78]

A is for AWAKENING

Once you awaken as a parent you will realize nothing but yourself affects you. Cain't nobody make you curse them out. You will no longer blame others for what constantly happens. Ain't nothing happening to YOU, it's just happening.

You can't continually degrade the person YOU decided to go half on a baby with. Wake up and smell the crack. You picked him or her and then moved them in with you. So kick yo' own ass then forgive yourself, the sperm or egg donor and then forgive this world.

Parenting is an acting job. I don't mean be phony with your children, they'll see right through you. However, we all know you have to sometimes be more interested, excited, and composed then you might very well want to be. You have to wear your mother

---

78 *Breath, shake, stretch, let it go*

PARENTHOOD VS. HOOD PARENT

or father hat at all times. You speak one way to your siblings and hopefully another to your parents. How do you talk to your kids? Your parenting has to be on point. You need a good game and/or poker face.

For instance, if your child says, "Ma, can I call my daddy and see if he's coming to my baseball game," you can't think out loud. Once you awaken you will have peace and understanding and you will understand that you're an actor/parent first. Therefore, you shouldn't tell your child the first ignent[79] thought that comes to your mind such as:

"You know damn well that black (white or Puerto Rican) bastard ain't coming to yo' damn game. Muthafuck his lame ass. His ass needs to step up to the plate and pay some damn child support before I send his ass to jail. A ninja ain't shit."

On the other hand, an awakened, responsible parent will say, *"Sure, baby. Call him and see if he would like to come, but don't be too disappointed if he can't make it."*

Your grief causes your child grief. Your tranquility will give your child peace and harmony. Allow your child to figure out their parent is a lame on their own.

You can make your child more aware by passing down your awareness. If you want to make your child more ignorant, then pass down your ignorance.

To make sure that your child becomes aware make sure they are aware that they are responsible for their own happiness. No man or woman can make them happy. Joy comes from within. Teach them how to create things that will bring them joy and joy to others, then they'll be doing God's work.

---

79   *Ignorant*

R is for RESPECT

If your children see you disrespect your mother or father, then your children will disrespect you. Why are you surprised? What defense will you use in order to get your children to respect you, besides cursing and recurrent ass whuppins?

This is the best defense you could have: "Have you ever seen me disrespect my parents? Then you better never disrespect me." What could be better than this defense? This is better than ass whuppins, and it saves you a ton of energy. Kids are not only listening to what you say, they are watching and recording what you do and then playing it back in front of you and when you are not around.

If you don't respect your children eventually they won't respect you. Spiritually you don't own your children and they don't belong to you. They come through you.

If you're fortunate, one day they will leave you and become what God has intended. Treat them with love, honor and respect and they'll never have an excuse to disrespect you. They need to respect others' property, space, and every living thing on the planet. As a result they will gain self-respect.

This may sound impossible, but by all means don't curse out your children or in front of your children. Now if you are a serial curser it may be easier for you to find Osama bin Laden.

Don't say you're trying to stop. Trying means not doing. This will take time for you. When I'm pushed to the limit I substitute "blank" for whatever I may be thinking.

For instance, "Shut the *blank* door now!" If the kids want to know what the "blank" means be creative tell them "*brown.*" By then, you've had a few seconds to calm down. Believe me this is tried and true. It won't be long before you're delivered from cursing your children out like a blank-blank.

PARENTHOOD VS. HOOD PARENT

The major problem is since there is no mother or father of the year award for you to compete for, your lack of parenting gets overlooked unless a dear friend or family member calls CPS on your blank.

Therefore, you wake-up every Mother's or Father's Day with your chest sticking out like you're Cliff or Clair Huxtable. And since people continue to say Happy Mother's and Father's Day to you each year, you never get the real wake up call that says;

"Damn! You're fuckin' your kids up emotionally, psychologically, physically and mentally. They won't grow up to be ish if you don't depart some Love, Compassion and Wisdom on them everyday of their lives so that they will be blessed with peace and understanding. Give your kids some food for their soul." Click

When a friend or family member does give you a parenting tip, the first words that pass through your, often-dry, cracked lips are "These my muthafuckin' kids. Mind yo muthafuckin' business!"

Umm, whenever you use muthafuckin as an adjective to describe your house, job, pet, clothes, shoes, car, drink, children or misplaced herb, i.e, - "Where my mutherfuckin weed at?" - this automatically qualifies you as a hood parent.

You don't have to repeat yourself over and over again when you tell your child to clean up. Here's an alternative. Call your child into the room and say to them "look in my eyes, read my mind" and whisper like a serial killer, "do it Now–now-now-now-now!"

Cursing out children is fucked up, even if it is the norm in your zip code. If you continue to do the same thing and expect a different result you might be stupid. And I say this with love.

E is for EMPOWER

All children need to be empowered, educated and enlightened. The secret that some parents never hear is: "This is your job and your responsibility."

Don't wait for your children to reach school age to be empowered, educated and enlightened. You are their primary caregiver and teacher. This is how confidence is built and maintained for a lifetime. Few children will become drug addicted even in adulthood if you give them a foundation of empowerment.

The question is can you empower a child if you are not empowered as a parent? Can a baby mama produce a Michelle or Barack Obama? Answer? Hell No. This is why we have generations of human beings with limited awareness and marginal thinking. The Blind (parents) are leading the blind (children).

This cycle will be broken once parents seek enlightenment. Then children will become empowered. You can become empowered and enlightened by having a mentor who is enlightened. This could be a parent, friend, educator or anybody you know who has sound judgment.

Empower your children by teaching them the value of education and teaching them the positive values discussed earlier. Then they will be empowered by achieving in school. When you positively reinforce their achievements, they will continue to seek knowledge.

You may have to become a "*momzilla*[80]" and choose your kid's friends because there are many kids in the public school system that don't give a damn about achievement.

---

80   *A mom who is involved in every aspect of their child's life aka a Jewish mother*

Make sure you and your kids are on the same page and understand that you are not raising the next pimp or stripper. You could be raising the next prez, so aim high.

It is also imperative that they learn the importance of treating others as they want to be treated. Remind them to ask themselves what God would do in any given situation. Therein lies your answer. Enlightenment will soon follow.

N is for NOW

If not NOW, when? When I was in college living on campus and my apartment needed cleaning at the same time I needed to study, I solved my problem by doing nothing. The sad part is I knew not doing either one didn't make no damn sense. The insane have insane thinking. It took me a while to figure out my problem hadn't been solved by doing nothing.

There is no time, but the present.

Many people don't read books because they don't believe they have the time. Many people don't accomplish several dreams because they don't believe they have the time. Some people believe time is an illusion.

Five minutes of good sex goes buy much faster than five minutes at the DMV. I don't have time to workout. I don't have time to visit. I don't have time to get a degree. Does a shark shit in the ocean? Then you have time.

There is no time but the present.

Allow me to introduce to you Donald Trump, Oprah Winfrey, and Martha Stewart. Google them if you want to see what they have had time to do in their lifetime and in a 24-hour day.

When I was pledging a fraternity in college the first thing we had to memorize was **Excuses**.

P.A.R.E.N.T.

EXCUSES

*Excuses are tools
used by the incompetent
used to build broken bridges
that lead to nowhere, Sir!*

Time is on your side, but when you have the collective thinking of the ignorant masses, nonsense can make sense to you. Your thoughts are not your own and not unique. Someone else already thought it and implanted their thoughts in your mind and now not only do you believe their thoughts, you believe they're yours.

For instance, you're a self-proclaimed "Paperchaser" or Golddigger. You weren't born with this shit in your head. You've got the Hood-Matrix to thank. Unplug from that shit.

People who think outside the bun are the pioneers, warriors and mavericks. Once you realize you are caught in the matrix you will awaken, unplug and begin to create like God created. This is why rebels, warriors, and mavericks achieve greatness in life. They don't think like the norm.

Harriet Tubman could have chosen to *trick for dollars*[81] at the local juke joint, instead she thought, "I can free enslaved Africans." And so she did.

John H. Johnson, publisher of Ebony and Jet Magazines, could have chosen to mack bitches and pimp hos. Instead, he dreamed of building an empire.

"I can build a publishing company." And so he did.

---

81   *Strip*

Robert Johnson, founder of BET, thought, "I can create a TV network." He could've settled for gambler or street huslah.

Barack Obama, thought, "I can be president of the United States." And so it is.

The universe will work with you if you stop working against it. Every achievement, small and great, begins with a thought. A thought the thinker turns into reality. You must believe in the possibility.

Now is the only time there is, so don't wait on the next lifetime to create. This used to be my mantra, "Don't put off 'till tomorrow what you can do the day after tomorrow." Yeah, I got issues.

You can't function in the past and you can't function in the future. The only time you can function is NOW. How will you use the time and space that has been given to you during your birth time on the planet?

When traces of the past or future come into your mind just press DELETE and don't give it a second thought. This is how you remain focused and present. PRESS DELETE. Accidents don't happen when you're present because it's then and only then you are totally aware of your surroundings.

Parents, what can you do now? Well, since now is the only time you have, focus on whatever it is you wish to accomplish and do it now.

Your children need you now. P.A.R.E.N.T them NOW.

T is for TEACH by EXAMPLE

Children aren't born ignorant or racist. This is learned behavior. Many kids get it from their parents.

What if you were a really wise person and decided to have children? Now, just think if the only thing you passed in school was gas, and decided to have children. You see how it works? You create what you are.

Sometimes an ignorant parent can work to certain children's advantage because the wise child will say, "Damn, I don't want to be nothing like that slack bastard when I grow up." As a result, they grow up and achieve greatness. However, this is the exception.

So, teach by example. Be the change you want to see on our planet. Road rage is taught and learned behavior. I make a habit not to look at idiots who are driving near me so I don't know if you flicked me off or not because I'm too busy texting.

Unfortunately, parents, unlike actors, don't get incentives to improve on their parenting game. Actors get paid millions for their performances. They get paid for pretending to be a parent on the TV screen, while many actual parents are rewarded with no child support every month.

I'm not blaming the actor, but dangling carrots such as awards and cash are what motivate most people to perform award winning work. There's no million dollar national parent-of-the-year awards show that gets televised annually.

Actors get Oscars, singers get Grammys, writers get Pulitzer prizes, athletes receive cash prizes and gold medals, and hood parents get arrested.

The secret is the parent and the child are the same person. Many people with arrested development procreate. Adults with childlike emotions are having kids. The only difference between children and many adults is kids can't vote.

Adults display the same behavior on the Interstate and at nightclubs that kids display on the playground in elementary school.

PARENTHOOD VS. HOOD PARENT

The Behavior	Kids	Adults
Cursing	✓	✓
Tell lies	✓	✓
Fighting	✓	✓
Flirting	✓	✓
Shoot Birds	✓	✓
Kill or die to be 1st in line	✓	✓

Many parents are no smarter than a 5th grader.

Some of us still solve problems like we did when we were 10. We throw tantrums, hit walls, slam doors and hit each other while in our 20s, 30s, 40s, 50s, and up.

The same shit that affects children affects adults: immaturity, tantrums, jealousy, crying, and lying. You name it and all this shit is happening in the workplace. Don't follow them home.

All this dysfunction gets passed down from generation to generation. Understand that you are at this moment in time for a reason. Time should be used as a learning mechanism in order to grow and develop emotionally, intellectually, and spiritually. So be the example you want to see.

TALK TIME

PARENTHOOD VS. HOOD PARENT

The only people that like to be heard more than barbers are children. We all know women like to be heard and many men wouldn't be offended if women chose to listen. But children need to be heard and listened to. They need quality time.

If you noticed, kids really want to be heard once you get on the phone or when you have company at the crib. But before you scream, "Go sit yo ass down, you see grown folks talkin!" you could think before you speak.

Most times children are just testing you to see where they rank on your level of importance. You could say, "Excuse me baby we're going to spend the rest of your childhood together. Let me talk on the phone. Thank you and good night." "Good night" always scares them.

Ask them, "Are you sleepy?"

When they lie and say, "No," say, "Me, too."

Whenever you pose questions surrounding bedtime they will quickly get *ghost*[82] on you. Humor is the biggest art and part of parenting, which will make your parenting job much easier. But many parents have not mastered the art of humor. Cursing and swearing is always an option, but it lacks the compassion and creativity that every child needs to grow and develop soundly.

Conversations are something that parents RARELY have with their children. In general, parents talk AT or TO their children not WITH their children. Often parents talk at each other. So the thought to have a conversation with your child never really crosses your mind.

So when you tell your child, "Get yo muthafuckin ass out that bed and wash the damn dishes like I told you. I aint gon tell you no

---

82   *To disappear*

damn mo," it sounds pretty ok to you. It even sounds normal to the child because it may be all they know.

Many parents don't know they can accomplish the same thing by saying, "Get up and wash the dishes before something bad happens to you, boo." Let the children use their imagination sometimes. This could mean several things like snatching their cell phone. This is the best way to improve grades and get chores done around the house. Of course, to you the threat could mean something violent and harmful, but no one has to know this but you.

Screaming, yelling, cursing, swearing, ranting, and raving gets old after awhile. It also tires you out. If you notice, the kids are calm most times. Meanwhile, you're the one buggin' out. Your pressure's up, you're getting more gray hair and before you know it you're having a stroke for dinner with a heart attack on the side.

Shock your children and sit down and have a conversation with them. Tell them what your expectations are and be consistent. Children love loopholes so you must learn to follow through AND follow up.

Children will respect you more if you respect them.

Kids in general can be obstinate. So you have to give them the business. If you tell them "no" and they begin to throw a tantrum at any age, get real close and place your hand on their shoulder or knee if you're sitting, look them in the eye and gently say, "Mommy's getting angry. Don't make mommy angry. If you make mommy angry, something bad is going to happen and you are going to be upset and perhaps limping in the end." Remind them love doesn't hurt, but ass whuppins do. They do forget sometimes.

It's OK to apply slight pressure to the shoulder or knee for effect so they can fill the tension and stress that is building. Remember to look in their eyes the entire time. It's even a good idea to include an involuntary tick that jerks your neck and shoulder in an insane manner every now and then. This takes the child's attention from the tantrum they were about to have and directs their attention to the mental breakdown you are currently having.

Invite them to go their room and come back when they're ready to have a conversation. If you never permit your children to throw tantrums as toddlers they won't continue to throw tantrums during adulthood.

You have to teach peace and understanding by example. If they see you curse out your family, spouse, friends on a regular basis, you're teaching them how to communicate. What you say at home they repeat at school. Don't be shocked or surprised when your kids get slick out the mouth. Their behavior has been learned and you are the teacher.

Make a pact with your family. "I won't call you no mo bitches. You don't call me no mo asshole muthafuckas. We will not yell and scream at each other." Make sure everyone is on the same page. Kids will be relieved to know their parents will never yell at them again. Believe that!

Teach them how to unlearn the 'hood' behavior. Tell them you take responsibility for mis-communicating to them in the past. Now, you both are going to learn how to have conversations together. After that, if your child raises his or her voice to you, have a seat in front of the computer, go online together with them and Google *foster care*.

UPWARD BOUND

PARENTHOOD VS. HOOD PARENT

I've heard it said that college ain't for everybody. But children ain't for everybody either. Yet, people who can't afford to take care of them and have no parenting skills keep popping them out like the old woman who lived in the freakin' shoe. One child is too many if you treat them like doo-doo.

I know some of you 30-year-old parents are thinking you're too old to go to college. "In four years I'll be 34." Well guess how old you'll be in 4 years if you don't go to college?

At least college is only a 4 year commitment. Children today are a lifetime commitment. Then you have to include the sperm donor or birth parent because they are going to be a part of your life at minimum a lifetime.

Do you have a desire for your children to attend a college or a university? If you do, it may be a good idea for you to register for some classes and get some higher learning instead of just getting higher. This is referred to as teaching by example.

I know some of you are thinking school ain't easy. Well neither is your life. Life is actually easy, but you rather make it hard. Don't allow the fear of getting a formal education hold you back. If you didn't pay attention in school, then your skills may be low. But if you're not slow you can learn anything you want. You learned how to pass drug tests while continuing to do drugs so you can pass any test you choose.

The ghetto is over-crowded because people find resting on their *laurels*[83] a favorite pastime. Don't watchin' movies on bootleg DVDs over and over again get old after a while?

Ninjas pride themselves on seeing movies repeatedly. "I saw Friday 99 times!" You shouldn't take pride in that. That's a damn shame.

---

83   Ass

Do the math. You watch a 2-hour movie 99 times. That's 198 hours. Add 10 hours for miscellaneous pauses, bathroom, telephone, and *ROTFLMMFAO*[84] breaks, and you've spent 208 hours on one ghetto movie.

Guess what? You're expected to study 3 hours a week per credit hour. This is why 12 hours per semester makes you a fulltime student. 12 X 3 = 36. That's 36 hours a week you should be in the books.

A semester lasts approximately 15 weeks. Multiply that times the 12 hours of class time you have each week and it equals about 180 hours of class time per semester. Therefore, we know one thing for sure you have time for college or professional training.

---

84 *Rolling on the floor, laughing my mutha fuckin' ass off*

WORK ETHNIC

WORK ETHNIC

In life you have careers and you have jobs. The basic difference between the two is a job can be shitty. You may work as a means to an end or until something better comes along.

A career is the shit. Retirement and pension are included. If you can earn a living doing what you enjoy the most, then you are creating like God intended and you are fortunate.

If you decide to have children it's a good idea if you work to support them. Remember you chose to get pregnant and / or you chose to remain pregnant.

Therefore, you will need a career to support your family. Careers usually require education or professional training. I would suggest you get educated or trained before you begin to have children. It might be hard to imagine, but childcare is higher than your baby daddy.

Don't say, "I can't afford childcare so I can't work. Say, "I can't afford children or childcare so I won't get pregnant." The major benefit in building your career first is you won't have to name your daughter, Paverty and your son, Jayle.

**GIVE
ME
CREDIT
OR
GIVE
ME
DEBT**

GIVE ME CREDIT OR GIVE ME DEBT

The truth is some people are born with the ability to manage money. The brother you called Stingy Benji now has established credit. The friend or relative who also saved their dirty ass candy necklace until it was mangy and brown, while you ate all of yours in one gulp may be debt free, too.

Some people save while others spend money before they get it. When two spenders unite you have the recipe for bankruptcy.

Having good credit is the spice of life. As a parent having good credit can change the trajectory of your life. "Yo air is in yo mama name" because you gotta closet full of Air Jordans.

You don't maintain good credit by just paying your bills. Paying your bills on time or BEFORE they're due is the secret. Every time you are late in a payment that is a strike against you. This gives credit cards companies the right to instantly raise your interest rate as high as 30%. Damn is right.

Just because you don't go to your mailbox don't mean the bills ain't there waiting for you. You can run from the bill collectors, but you can't hide from your bills. If you find opening bills very stressful, then stop creating bills, big baller and lil' mama.

Stop getting pissed when bill collectors call you for money you owe. Having your children lie saying you ain't home is scandalous. Stop teaching your children how to lie. Allow them to learn on their own. I know bill collectors like to get slick-out-the-mouth.[85] I always talked to my bill collectors, but they would eventually hang up on me.

You knew you couldn't afford that flat screen when you bought it. Trying to keep up with the Jacksons, Jenkins, Joneses, and Combes is bananas.

---

85   *Rude and discourteous*

Credit cards can be your best friend. They can help you establish credit. They can also be your worst nightmare. Experts say anything below 15% interest with rewards is good for college students. For someone with good to excellent credit, anything below 13% interest with rewards would be considered good.

Bad credit is a b!tch. So make sure your credit, and who ever you choose to procreate with, has good credit.

According to Fair Issac, more commonly referred to as FICO, the average credit score in the United States is 723 on a scale of 850. Fair Isaac is the main credit-scoring model that most all creditors use; here is their credit-scoring breakdown:

SUPER KOOL

700 and above – Very good to excellent. Lenders will have no problems giving you a loan at a low interest rate with a credit score of 700 or above.

GOOD & PLENTY

680 to 699 – This credit score puts you in the "Good" category. That one point between good and very good to excellent credit generally makes little difference to lenders so don't sweat it.

PRETTY OK

620 to 679 – If your credit score falls into this range, you fall into the "Okay" category. The closer your score is to 679, the better. 620 is considered to be a "par" credit rating and you may be required to provide supporting information such as additional income statements, personal and professional references as well as documentation confirming time at your current job.

DAMN, DAMN, DAMN

580 to 619 – While you aren't in the "Bad" category yet, you are leaning on the edge if your credit score falls in this range. 620 is the prime rate cut-off, so plan on paying a higher interest rate.

HOLLA BACK

500 to 580 – You can still get credit in this scoring range, but expect to pay a very high interest rate and look closely at the terms of your agreement. Closely examine how your interest rate is calculated. Some predatory lenders will charge interest rates on car loans that are calculated like credit cards, on a daily average balance. If you see these words in your disclosures for a car loan, drop the pen and holla back.

WTF

499 and below – Yes, even with a score of 499 or below you can still be extended credit, but the interest rates will kill you financially. Take a year or two to pay off your collections or bad debt, clean up your credit and reapply at a later date. In other words, holla back.

A Vantage credit score rating scale on the other hand, has scores ranging from 501 to 990. It simultaneously grades the individual on a letter scale of A to F. It is claimed as being superior to FICO, leading to a uniform credit score rating by all the three agencies.

The Vantage system has 501 as the lowest rating ranked F. A score of 990 is the highest and is ranked an A. The entire Vantage credit score rating scale is as follows:

    901 to 990 – A
    801 to 900 – B
    701 to 800 – C
    601 to 700 – D
    501 to 600 – F

EGO,
BODY,
& SPIRIT

EGO

The mind is where the ego presides. The mind has a tendency to create how it was created. So if you were raised around drama it tends to attract drama. This has you convinced that you are it and it is you. If you run from drama and drama finds you, then you're running from yourself. You are the common denominator. You gotta big ego. If you're defensive, you're defending your ego. Let it die. Kill it wit a skillet.

Treat others as you want to be treated –

DO YOU KNOW ANYONE WHO PRACTICES THIS ON A DAILY BASIS?

Are you consistently doing it? Why not? Why are you allowing your ego to stop you from doing it? Why are you allowing your ego to control you? This is Scripture. There is strength in kindness.

Your ego has got it twisted and you convinced. This is why it's easier for some to say "I hate you" and much more difficult to say "I love you."

Being in a physical body can be deceiving and lead to deception. You begin to feel separated from the bodies around you. But if we are spiritual beings having a human experience then this could be considered the dream Dr. King spoke about.

We all have a dream. We are all living our dream. Life is but a dream. Even if your dream is a living nightmare, you created it. Your ego helped get you where you are.

Does he like me? Should I steal it? Should I kill him for what he did to me?

Ain't nobody did nothing to you. Think of yourself as the presence behind the projector in the movie theater. The movie you see is the movie you are projecting. You create the film. You are the source of what you see on the screen. The projector (your mind) just shines the light that reflects what's playing in your head. You are the observer.

Therefore, nothing is happening TO you. It's just happening. Don't allow your ego to get it twisted. So if somebody yells at you on the road and says, "Fuck you, you non-driving bitch!" you can say, "Jesus take the wheel," get out and commence to whuppin their ass as your ego would have you do. Or you could look straight ahead and ask yourself, "What would God do?" Remember your kids are watching.

Once you get above the repetitive thoughts constantly bombarding your mind and become still and quiet, peace and understanding will come. Trust and believe.

BODY

As a parent you have to set the example for your children. Gentlemen, always remember "Healthy-mind/healthy-body." Medical experts recommend your waistline be under 36 inches. If you and your wife or yo baby mama are having twins and nobody can tell who's carrying them, that's a problem. If you look down and you can't see your one eyed monster, that's a bigger problem. If your partner can't see it then it's a major problem.

Ladies, medical experts recommend your waistline be under 33 inches. This includes all women under the rainbow, but I want my Latina mamis to read this carefully because living in Miami I see a lot of flesh that the general public and I don't really deserve to see.

If low-rise jeans and half tops make you look like a muffin top – that's not a good look, ma. Your stretch marks are intended for you, your man and your immediate families viewing pleasure only.

EGO, BODY, & SPIRIT

Parents, have you noticed that you're not the only one in your family who is obese. Take a look at your children. Childhood obesity has tripled in the last 20 years. Your children are obese because you have continually fed them the wrong shit for far too long. I understand they eat what you eat, but that's the problem not a defense.

I understand it takes practice to work on mind, body and spirit simultaneously, however, start now on this journey.

I can remember when I would tell myself, "I'm going to workout 4 days a week." Monday would come and I wouldn't be trying to workout no 4 days a week so guess how many I did? Yep, Zip. My rocket science knowledge kicked in and said, "Well you can't do 4 days so you can't do none." Just ignent.

Then I said to myself one day is better than no day. Before I knew it I was working out three to four days a week. I'd work out Monday, Tuesday, Wednesday, and Thursday. Sometimes I wouldn't make it past Wednesday, but it was cool because I had already done three days so if I wanted to sit on my ass the rest of the week and weekend I could. I would just start back again on Monday. Now if you are a person who gains weight when or if you dream about food then you may need to eat less and move more to get you cardio on. Walking is the best-kept secret.

Don't reward your negative behavior. If you didn't meet your workout goals for the week, then why are you *maxin*[86] on desserts? Don't treat yourself if you don't deserve to be treated. Eat to live; don't live to eat. Check out or Google: The Daniel Fast if you really want to get the entire family's health in check. I wasn't born with this body.

---

86 *Grubbing, throwing down or indulging on foods*

SPIRIT

Spiritually, I began reading more enlightened authors and this empowered me. I began to put to practice what I had been reading. I also realized that if you read a spiritual book by a great author and don't have a spiritual awakening then you didn't get it. You are not awakened. It's nothing forced, you simply awaken once you put your ego to sleep for good.

Your spiritual journey is the most important trip you will ever take. It will require spiritual reading and practice. Some of the greatest spiritual minds on the planet have written books to help you gain a higher level of spiritual awareness and higher level of consciousness.

What does this really mean?

It means NOT living in the PAST or for the FUTURE. Focus on this moment. Use your memory to remember GOD, not bullshit. Press **DELETE** when you start thinking about shit that don't really matter. Then empty the **TRASH** to get rid of bad memories. The brain works like a computer.

As the world turns remember to use time for its given purpose – unlearning, healing, learning. When you take time out to worry and to have fear you are not AWAKE. Your mind is somewhere in the past or future. It's not possible to fear and worry and BE in the present moment. You have to be worrying about something in the past or future or fearing something from the past or in the future.

Think about it this way. When you are daydreaming (this is always about a past or future moments in time) you are not "in the now." You are not conscious of your surroundings. That's why someone has to snap you out of it and bring you back to the PRESENT. The mind is a terrible thing to lose.

The only thing worry and fears does is cause stress and/or cause you to kill or be killed. Worry and fear don't solve problems. Peace and understanding solves problems and you gain peace and understanding by surrendering and embracing this thing called LIFE, not by going against it.

A great book to read is *A Course In Miracles*. If you read it and then don't use love, compassion and wisdom when making all decisions, then you didn't get it. Continue studying.

Ultimately, you want to begin working on mind, body, and spirit simultaneously. God knows you got time. So whenever this physical world gets you down grab a book and do some soul searching. The answers are in black and white.

You weren't born to die.

You were CREATED to live.

HOPE
IS
DOPE

HOPE IS DOPE

"Train up a child in the way he should go, and when he is old he will not depart from it."
~ **Proverbs**

The hope is parents will begin to awaken and discover the children they are raising are merely a reflection of the parenting that is taking place. Hope, dreams, and change now have a whole new meaning. I'm talking about a meaning you can touch if you can get past the secret service. President Barack Obama and the First Lady are real. They took the hood out of hood parent. They are the NEW BLACK. The secret: they didn't have hood parents. They realized that there was more room at the top than there is at the bottom and strived for excellence instead of becoming statistics.

Change has come. The dream is now a reality. And the time is NOW. What changes have you made? What changes are you willing to make? Everything must change. Love your children. Show them you love them and tell them you love them. Now.

Drama, anxiety and ego are being replaced with Love, Compassion and Wisdom, which will lead to peace and understanding for you and your children. We're all pieces of the dream.

You are the **WAY**.

This is the **TRUTH**.

Can you see the **LIGHT**?

It's time *for* CHANGE and it's time *to* CHANGE.

God Bless the Child.

I'm Benn Setfrey and I approve this message.

AND THE AWARD GOES TO...

THE AWARD GOES TO...

PARENT OF THE YEAR AWARD

The Parent of the Year Award goes to Mr. Richard Williams and Ms. Oracene (Price) Williams. They are the proud parents of Venus and Serena Williams and a few more. They married in 1980 and divorced in 2002. The Williams are proof you can be from the ghetto and not of the ghetto. Salute!

www.ingramcontent.com/pod-product-compliance
Lightning Source LLC
Chambersburg PA
CBHW051755040426
42446CB00007B/375